Maximize Your School Marketing

Johanna M. Lockhart

ROWMAN & LITTLEFIELD
Lanham • Boulder • New York • London

Published by Rowman & Littlefield
A wholly owned subsidiary of The Rowman & Littlefield Publishing Group, Inc.
4501 Forbes Boulevard, Suite 200, Lanham, Maryland 20706
www.rowman.com

Unit A, Whitacre Mews, 26-34 Stannary Street, London SE11 4AB

British Library Cataloguing in Publication Information Available

Library of Congress Cataloging-in-Publication Data
Names: Lockhart, Johanna M., 1943– author.
Title: Maximize your school marketing / Johanna M. Lockhart.
Description: Lanham : Rowman & Littlefield, a wholly owned subsidiary
   of The Rowman & Littlefield Publishing Group, Inc., [2016]
Identifiers: LCCN 2016027094 (print) | LCCN 2016040270 (ebook) |
   ISBN 9781475829983 (cloth : alk. paper) | ISBN 9781475829990 (pbk. : alk. paper) |
   ISBN 9781475830002 (electronic)
Subjects: LCSH: Education—Marketing. | Schools—Public relations. |
   Educational fund raising.
Classification: LCC LB2847 .L65 2016 (print) | LCC LB2847 (ebook) |
   DDC 371.19/5—dc23
LC record available at https://lccn.loc.gov/2016027094

♾ ™ The paper used in this publication meets the minimum requirements of American
National Standard for Information Sciences—Permanence of Paper for Printed Library
Materials, ANSI/NISO Z39.48-1992.

Printed in the United States of America

Maximize Your School Marketing

Contents

Preface

Several years ago, at the request of school administrators in the Houston Independent School district, I created a workshop, *Marketing Your School*. The administrators who attended were aware that the landscape for public schools was changing, and they wanted practical tools and skills to control the new environment rather than be controlled by it.

The success of the *Marketing Your School* workshops led to a subsequent program, *Building Beneficial Partnerships*. As I conducted these workshops over several years, participants repeatedly expressed a desire for a user-friendly guidebook to help them as they implemented their marketing and public relations initiatives.

Four years ago I wrote *How to Market Your School* to meet that need. Subsequent phone calls and e-mails from individuals who had purchased my book made it clear to me that, in addition to public schools, private, charter, faith-based, and international schools also found the book useful for developing and improving their marketing skills. I also realized that my book was now more than four years old and in need of updating, especially in the area of utilizing technology and social media to market more effectively.

A final consideration was to make the book more affordable to schools by creating two books: one for schools wishing to create and maintain a marketing program and one for schools wanting to enhance the effectiveness of an existing one.

Fundamentals of School Marketing covers marketing fundamentals and marketing communication. This book is designed to help schools establish and maintain a marketing program. The marketing communication chapter covers the essential elements of effective communication, a component essential to successful marketing. *Maximize Your School Marketing* covers the fundamentals of media, community, and public relations, fund-raising, and social media. This book is designed to enhance an existing marketing program through greater internal and external outreach efforts.

I wish to address the needs of all types of schools. If it sometimes seems that I have given public schools more attention, it is simply because they vastly outnumber other types of schools and, more importantly, they are not as practiced in the art of school marketing as private, charter, or faith-based schools.

The present environment for all types of schools is more competitive than in the past. Schools are competing not only for students but also for teachers, administrators, and community support. Students, parents, employees, and members of the community are now "customers" who can choose to attend, work in, and support a school or not. Their choices are determined by how they view education in general and their local schools in particular. Marketing, communication, and public relations help shape those views.

Successfully marketing a school involves a concerted effort that includes public relations, media relations, relationship management, and communication. However, often school administrators are not familiar with these fields. Do not despair. The information in *Fundamentals of School Marketing* can help you get started. If you already have a marketing effort, *Maximize Your School Marketing* will facilitate enhancement of what you are already doing. Whatever your goals are, I hope one or both these books will become worn from use.

Acknowledgments

I extend my sincere gratitude to those who shared their time, talents, knowledge, and experiences with me.

Hector Rodríguez, Principal, John Herrera Elementary School, Houston, Texas

R. Neal Wiley, Fine Arts Director, Houston Independent School District

Joanie Haley, Executive Director, McNair Foundation

Elaine Naleski, Director of Community Relations, Colorado Springs School District 11

Special appreciation and thanks to Carol Marcott, a treasured friend, a supportive mentor, a wise advisor, and a motivating cheerleader, and to my son, John Lockhart, who has assisted me in immeasurable ways to make this second addition and my website possible.

Introduction

The purpose of *Maximize Your School Marketing* is to give school administrators, who have already initiated a school marketing program, additional knowledge and tools to enhance their efforts. School marketing basics, covered in the companion book, *Fundamentals of School Marketing*, can be further developed through improved media relations, community outreach, social media, public relations, and fund-raising.

Most of this book's content is presented through succinct explanations of the many ways that administrators can develop, implement, and maintain an ongoing marketing program to promote their schools internally and externally. I chose this format because administrators in my workshops indicated that they do not have time to read the traditional text format to extract ideas and activities they can use. Having the information in manageable "chunks" they could read quickly was appealing.

The latest technology can be a blessing or a curse for school administrators. *Maximize Your School Marketing* begins with "Technology and Social Media," a detailed approach to improving communication with students, parents, teachers, and the community by integrating technology and social media into the marketing effort. The growing importance of technology in marketing demands a chapter devoted to using multiple channels as a means to foster effective two-way communication. Careful consideration of technology and social media and how to use it will eliminate much of the angst associated with it.

Many public school administrators, with some justification, do not look upon the media as an ally or even a benign necessity but rather as a propagator of negative hype. Private schools may not receive as much scrutiny as public

1

schools, but often they do not receive as much positive exposure. This need not be the case. A proactive approach to working with the media can generate positive stories about your school and mitigate negativity if there is a crisis. Chapter 2, "Media Relations," offers advice on creating positive relationships with the media and, if necessary, how to respond when faced with a crisis.

Decreasing resources and increasing needs require that many schools look to external sources for assistance. Chapter 3, "Building Community Partnerships," addresses the question I hear from so many school administrators: "How can I develop and maintain successful relationships with external partners?"—namely, businesses and nonprofit organizations. This chapter includes a mutually beneficial approach plus support materials for initiating, developing, and maintaining good external relationships that can improve the learning environment for all children.

Chapter 4, "Public Relations, Inside and Out," describes how to build positive internal and external relationships. Included is a variety of activities to enhance the marketing effort. Incorporate these activities into your plans as time and resources permit.

All schools, even the most affluent, participate in some kind of fund-raising. The need for raising funds ranges from providing school scholarships to providing more than the basic essentials. Fund-raising can be a chore for school staff, students, and parents. There seems to be no end to the number of fund-raising programs companies promote to schools. Chapter 5, "Fund-Raising," offers suggestions for assessing fund-raising programs and ways to mitigate the headaches that often accompany fund drives.

The success stories at the end of the book offer valuable insight from education administrators who have been successful in marketing-related initiatives and were willing to share their experiences and expertise. I have included their stories not only to serve as real-life examples but also to inspire and motivate.

For those who wish to fine-tune their marketing, a companion book, *Fundamentals of School Marketing*, offers a guide to developing and implementing a marketing plan, conducting market research, and maintaining a database to enhance marketing efforts and effective marketing communication.

ABOUT THE AUTHOR

Since I will be guiding you through the marketing process, you may want to know something about me. I have over 15 years of experience in marketing and public relations in private sector that run the gamut from regional director for a public relations firm that represented resort conference centers to director of marketing for an investment firm that specialized in oil and gas securities. What I came to realize is that, no matter what the industry, the underlying marketing principles are the same.

For more than ten years, as manager of marketing and client relations in the Office of Marketing and Business Development at the Houston Independent School District, I had the opportunity to apply those principles to the department's marketing efforts and to develop marketing workshops for schools. To date, I have presented the *Marketing Your School* and the *Building Beneficial Partnerships* workshops to more than a thousand school administrators. In addition, I have spoken on school marketing at state and national conferences.

In 2014, I retired from the school district and am now launching a new endeavor. My website, marketyourschool.net, is a result of feedback from readers of the first edition of my book. It will allow me to provide the assistance to schools—public, private, charter, or parochial—anywhere in the country or abroad. The goal is to provide more assistance in different mediums and be more interactive with schools that realize the benefits of marketing.

My academic career includes a bachelor of arts in languages and a master of arts in communication. As an undergraduate student, I had the opportunity to study in Mexico, Spain, Germany, and England. My experiences in other countries made me acutely aware of the importance of recognizing, understanding, and respecting the differences that exist between groups while utilizing the commonalities to mutual advantage. Through my professional and academic experiences, I have become convinced that knowing your various audiences and being able to communicate with a valid knowledge of *their* expectations is key to successful marketing.

Chapter 1

Technology and Social Media

The opportunities and challenges technology presents to school marketers have changed dramatically. At one time, the challenge was largely access to technology and training employees in the fundamentals of use. Many schools needed help with the basics of creating a website, integrating e-mail into school communications, and establishing a consensus that technology was a valuable use of resources.

Today, the challenges revolve more around strategy, planning, and simply not being overwhelmed by the many new channels of communications. Technologies for engaging students, parents, the community and faculty have dramatically decreased in price and dramatically increased in ease of use. This demands that schools seriously consider which technology will benefit them and which will not.

SOCIAL MEDIA

It seems everyone is talking about tweets, blogs, and wikis. And the speed at which new products and terminology are added can seem intimidating. But, you don't have to be a techno wiz to enjoy the significant benefits of social media. Today, a person without an information technology background can acquire a domain name, create a website, set up e-mail and a blog, and have a Facebook page and a Twitter account at the ready, all within a couple of hours and at a cost of under a hundred dollars.

What does the term "social media" mean? When we hear the word *media*, most of us think of *the* media, that is, the newspaper, radio, television,

Internet, and other sources through which we receive daily news and information. A medium, however, is any channel through which communication is transmitted. Watercooler gossip, artworks, and opinion papers are all different forms of channels or media. Social media uses technology to create a variety of new channels to communicate.

The key characteristic of any social interaction is sharing news, ideas, values, opinions, and knowledge. Social media uses technology to greatly expand who, how, and when individuals and organizations can share these same kinds of things. So, social media might be defined as a variety of technology-based channels through which we can share information with others quickly.

Social media is becoming a valuable marketing tool. If your competition is not already using social media, it is likely they soon will. Many of the students you wish to attract and retain accept it as a normal means of communication; so, it is an effective way to reach them. And, like much of today's technology, its influence is going to increase.

At the same time, however, this favorable trend also complicates the marketing equation. While technologies have become cheaper and easier to use, new channels, particularly social media, have changed the behavior and expectations of students, parents, and faculty. Social media has made having a conversation about your school simpler in many ways but more complex in some ways.

There are now more channels to communicate with your community than your school could practically keep up with, and benefits and implications of using each are different. The good news is that with good planning and informed use, you can play on the strengths of each platform to reduce your overall marketing effort and reap benefits you couldn't have anticipated. For example, regular updates to a school Facebook page can be a simpler alternative to maintaining a blog. A Twitter feed can be used as part of a faculty recruitment plan. A YouTube channel can help potential students and new faculty find your school through searches while making it simpler to publish authentic content from your students and faculty.

Social media also facilitates two-way communication. To be effective, a marketing strategy requires insight regarding what people think about your school. What they think may be positive or negative, it may be based on inaccurate or incomplete information, but it is what they are thinking nevertheless, and you need to know about it.

Accordingly, social media needs to be at the forefront of your technology planning. While it might be tempting for school administrators to view it as a fad, a burden, and a distraction, social media has fundamentally changed how conversations about products and services occur. At the same time, planning it into your marketing creates opportunities to reduce the effort it takes to create awareness, address community concerns, and recruit new students and faculty.

Social media gives your school or district a variety of ways to respond to information, misinformation, or lack of information quickly and extensively. A common complaint of school administrators about traditional news media is the limited ability of the school or district to respond to negative or inaccurate stories and to get greater exposure of the positive news about their schools in a timely manner. Instead of writing a rebuttal letter to the local newspaper with the hope that it is published or depending on visits to the school's website to read about your accomplishments, you can use social media to communicate your message quickly and directly to a large group of people.

With more schools and educational resources online, school marketers also need an awareness of increasing their school's visibility in search and social media. Having a website that tells a compelling story about your school is fundamental but of little value if it can't raise visibility in search and social media. While you may be pleased with your school's website, it means very little if potential students and faculty never find you on the web. The Internet is immense and as vast as the ocean. Search engines do a good job of helping people find you, but, even in a small market, you are competing with more schools than ever before for the eyes of your potential customers. Taking this even further, the attention span and habits of your customers have changed too.

Search is important, but not exclusively through search engines. Search occurs on many platforms, and your community wants to be engaged with a steady stream of easily consumable social media. Accordingly, techniques and practices for increasing search and social media visibility need to be in the forefront of the minds of school marketers.

With these considerations in mind, this chapter is designed to help you plan a simple and coordinated marketing effort that encompasses your website, e-mail, and social media. Assuming that your school already has a web presence and e-mail, this chapter will help you devise and implement a plan that will:

- Help your school be more visible in search results.
- Create a sustainable process for publishing content.
- Help you be proactive in social media conversations important to your school.
- Achieve greater student and faculty involvement.
- Improve faculty recruitment.
- Help you use content in the right channels.
- Help you measure the effectiveness of your marketing initiatives.

YOUR WEBSITE

This chapter will not cover the various ways you can create a website. The goal of this chapter is to help you use your website in conjunction with social media tools to develop a coordinated, effective, measurable, and sustainable marketing presence on the Internet.

If your school is like most, it already has a website. Your school may have set it up on its own or with the help of volunteers, or your school may have a site maintained by your district. Regardless of how it was established, your school probably has something.

If your school has not yet set up a website, the process is simple, and there are many guides that cover that process better, and in more detail, than what can be discussed in this chapter. If you need some guidance and starting points for setting up a website, you should look first at one of the popular web publishing platforms. One of the best, most popular, and well-documented publishing platforms is Wordpress. Every technique or feature covered in this chapter and much more can be implemented in Wordpress. Even better, Wordpress is also free. Learn more at www.wordpress.org.

SEO CONSIDERATIONS

One theme of this chapter is that for your website, and other web marketing assets, you are designing for two audiences. One audience is your school's community, the current and potential students, parents, and faculty looking for information. The other audience is the search engines, such as Google, Bing, and Yahoo, which make your school visible in search results. While the community is the primary audience you serve, having a well-designed page that performs well in searches is key to creating new awareness of your school.

The design and content of your site can be optimized so that your school's web presence will show up higher in these search results. This practice is called search engine optimization, or SEO.

The good news is that the things you will need to do to serve each audience are largely one and the same. Search engines' first and foremost concern is delivering results that are

a. relevant
b. high quality

When search engines scour the Internet, indexing its content to build search results, they employ complex and highly evolved algorithms to determine what pages are best based on a set of assumptions about the searcher's intent. In line with the goal of delivering relevant and high-quality results, search engines identify and exclude pages that are deceptive, spam, or just simply of poor quality. As a school you are in an enviable position. Your site may be the official page of an institution. A "vital" search results in search engine vernacular. Your domain name, content, and the structure of your site are distinct from sites with a commercial intent. Accordingly, with little or no effort, your site will perform well when your potential audience is searching for your specific school or schools by district. One goal of this chapter is to help your school be a more relevant result in a wide variety of searches. For example, it would be fortunate if the potential student, parent, or faculty would searched for "Maria Montessori Academy." However, the reality is that the audience you want to reach will most likely be conducting searches such as follows:

"montessori schools san antonio"
"montessori school alamo heights"
"best montessori san antonio"
"private school alamo heights"
"montessori schools"

Through the techniques you will learn in this chapter, your school will become more visible in these searches, not only through search engines but also through social media channels where search and visibility are just as important for your school. If you simply reflect on where you are finding the educational information and content, search engines are important, but you probably become aware of more through social media. One of the lessons of this chapter is treating social media with equal importance and using it in ways that will also help your website's visibility in search.

The following are some types of social media and how your school or district might use them.

USING SOCIAL MEDIA CHANNELS

A Website Blog   Level of effort: Moderate   Value: High

While often categorized as a type of social media, a blog is better thought of as an extension of your website. While Facebook and Twitter are more suited to short updates and pointers to other content, blogs are suited for more long-form articles. Coverage of a new school program, a new faculty announcement, or a recap of a major school event are examples of the kinds of articles the blogs are well suited for.

Besides the information a blog can communicate to your community, blogs are effective in raising visibility for your school's website in two ways:

1. Blogs raise your website's rank in search engine results by providing continually updated and keyword-rich content on your website. This kind of content is what search engines like Google take into consideration most when judging how relevant and important a website is to a search a user makes on the web.
2. Blog posts provide content that can be linked back to from Facebook, Twitter, and other websites. These links, from referring websites, give your web page more direct visibility on these other websites and social media channels. However, they also are taken into consideration by search engines. Links back to your site from other websites indicate to search engines that your site is regarded as an authority with authentic content and information. Consequently, search engines will rank your website higher in search results.

Decide on the purpose of your blog. Is it to communicate with employees, exchange information with educators in other parts of the country, keep in touch with volunteers, or build two-way communication with parents, students, and the community? Departments within your district or school may choose to establish their own blogs:

- The community relations department could keep in touch with the business community or school volunteers.
- The department in charge of bond expenditures could keep contractors, parents, and the community updated on the progress of new construction and school renovations.
- The government relations department can report about the ongoing legislative session and the impact of legislation on schools.
- The superintendent or other administrators can report from conferences they are attending.
- School board members can communicate with their constituents.
- Schools and districts can take a proactive approach to bullying by clarifying district and school policies, allowing parents and students to express their concerns or ask questions, providing information to help parents and teachers detect when a student is a bully or is the target of bullying, and providing a channel for anyone to report incidents of bullying.

Once you have created a blog post, be sure to create tweets and Facebook posts that include links to your blog posts. Very few users may take the time to check your blog for new information, but many more will get passive updates through Facebook and Twitter.

Write your blog posts to include keywords based on terms you expect members of your community and potential students, faculty and parents to use when searching for information on schools like yours. If your school is a charter, private, or magnet school in a particular region or area of a city, aim to use those descriptors into your blog posts. For example, if your school is a charter school in the Heights neighborhood of Houston, try to incorporate references in your blog posts like "As a charter school in Houston's Heights area . . ." Research the terms used on websites frequented by the audiences you want to attract to your school. Look at your competitors' websites and marketing materials. You can also conduct keyword research by using search terms you anticipate will be used by your audience and seeing which bring up the results that most closely match your school. Keyword research tools can be found on the web but are of questionable value.

Below are some additional suggestions:

- Make it easy to find information by organizing it into categories.
- Use reverse chronology so that the newest information is easy to find at the top of the blog.
- The same rules for effective communication apply to blogs. Write short sentences. Avoid long paragraphs, jargon, and acronyms.
- Use headers.
- Create a clutter-free look.
- Post comments that create interest, offer information, spark debate, and bring people back for more.
- Offer lots of links (to other blogs, news articles, videos, and websites). One reason people will visit your blog is to find these links without having to search for them.
- Keep your blog current.

Much of the web is reputation based. More than what you say about yourself, search engines care about what others say about you. Links from other websites to yours are tracked by search engines and signal that your site is a trusted authority.

Facebook   Level of effort: High   Value: High

Its sheer ubiquity and the network effect of social media make Facebook one of the most effective tools for engaging a community that already has an awareness of your school. Community members may not check your school website often enough to be aware of events, announcements, and other news. Facebook, like Twitter, takes care of this by making your school a part of community members' daily social media diet. Similarly, Facebook activity can also be an outlet for content that does not merit blog posts or website updates. Like Twitter, it's also simpler and faster than updating a website.

Because it is so well suited to shorter and more informal content, Facebook posts can take the place of much of your blogging activity. Reserve blog entries for longer-form and more infrequent posts and use Facebook more often for regular updates events and news. However, don't forget to share links to blog posts on Facebook.

While the value of a Facebook page is very high, it also takes more maintenance than a blog or website. Followers of your Facebook page can share and comment on your posts. While this gains you much more real-time exposure, you also need to have someone assigned to moderate comments and respond to any negative feedback.

One way your school could use Facebook is to create a page for your school mascot. Post the mascot's picture, give him/her/it a persona, and then use the site to:

- Celebrate accomplishments
- Share photos of recent events
- Take fun and serious polls
- Let students know about events and opportunities outside the school
- Show video clips of school events
- Use the bulletin board for announcements and reminders
- Post links to interesting and informative sites

Twitter   Level of effort: Moderate   Value: High

Twitter is the social media platform that allows you to post updates in 140-character tweets. While newcomers to your school are more likely to visit and browse a Facebook page, Twitter activity will be dominated by the members who subscribe to your Twitter feed. Less of an outreach to the wider community, Twitter is a more effective tool for engagement with your current community of students, faculty, and parents. Twitter is ideal for timely news and updates about your school and its events, and it is an excellent way to create more connection and intimacy with the community that is already involved with your school.

Some of the ways you can use Twitter are as follows:

- Send reminders about
  - school or district events such as board meetings, community forums, school's open house, festivals, performances, sporting events, and so on;
  - testing periods; and
  - early school dismissals.
- Announce awards and accomplishments of students, teachers, schools, and the district.
- Communicate with alumni.
- Send alerts about news items related to your school or district that will appear on local television stations or in newspapers.
- Issue weather alerts affecting the schools.
- Send links to the following:
  - weekly or monthly online newsletter
  - district or school-related news items
  - videos of speeches by board members, superintendent, and others
  - photo pages
  - pending legislation you want the public to know about and respond to

There are ways that tweets can gain more visibility and exposure for your school. Twitter users can re-tweet what you post through your Twitter account. This is essentially like sharing a Facebook post and can gain visibility through the network effect of social media. For this reason, one of the best uses of Twitter is to socialize your other content, blog posts, Facebook posts, and YouTube videos. Few users may subscribe to a YouTube channel, but many more will follow you on Twitter to Facebook. Use channels like Facebook and Twitter to get more visibility for your school by posting uplinks to content that will keep them interested in your feed.

Twitter users also search for content of interest using hashtags. These tags are essentially keywords preceded in the tweet by the "#" symbol. Twitter users interested in schools like yours may find your Twitter feed via hashtags such as the following:

#montessoritexas
#charterschool
#sanantonioschool

Users searching for hashtags you use will find your tweets and may subscribe to your feed or follow links back to your school. Naturally, hashtags beg the question of which terms you should use in your tags. You may be familiar with so-called "hashtag abuse" in which Twitter users create hashtags that are intended more for emphasis than search value—for example,

#ihaterushhourtraffic. These tags are emotive but have no value in helping people find information about your school through Twitter.

Use common sense, but also consider using some of the free tools that can help you pick the best hashtag terms. The website www.hashtags.org is a free web service that allows you to see the frequency of use of any hashtag term you enter. Pick hashtags in use that most closely reflect your school and the content of your tweets.

Once you have a set of hashtags, try to standardize their use among your team. Facebook now also supports hashtags in posts. They perform the same search function and you should try to use many of the same tags you use for Twitter.

With these considerations in mind, a good tweet would have a format like the following:

San Antonio Montessori Job Fair http://bityurl.com #montessori #sanantonioschool

You may notice in the text of the tweet that the web link is very short. One handy tool for tweets is the use of a link shortener. Link shorteners take a long link and give you back a short link that points to the same web resource. These are handy for tweets since they save you more of the precious 140 characters.

You can even find out what people are saying about the school or district. Twitter has a search engine that lets you monitor what people are saying about any person or organization. This is a good way to determine the public's views about district initiatives, reaction to news items, and misperceptions that may be in the community.

One of the best ways to learn about the many features of social networking sites is to create one for yourself.

YouTube   Level of effort: Moderate   Value: High

For your school, the most obvious use of YouTube is creating a sense of community. Videos of sports, special events, and other school activities are an easy and entertaining way to engage your community of students, parent, and faculty.

What is not as obvious is that YouTube videos, particularly videos hosted as part of a YouTube channel, can give much greater visibility to your school outside your existing community. YouTube videos appear as part of search results in search engines such as Google and Bing. This gives your school the opportunity to appear more prominently in a wide variety of searches.

When thinking about video content, you should also be thinking about videos that highlight specific programs, aptitudes, and features of your school. These videos can be designed to attract prospective faculty as well as students. For example, if your school has developed a special academic program, let's say a program in math or science, you can have videos for those programs appear in search results for relevant keywords. Videos that highlight your school's excellence in specific academic areas or teaching methodologies can help your faculty and student recruitment efforts in addition to creating a sense of community around your school.

YouTube also allows you to set up a YouTube channel that organizes your videos and makes it simple for viewers of one video to find others as well as subscribe to be notified about new videos you post to you channel.

Like blog articles, YouTube videos have places for tags that help define search terms for the videos as well as a description and a category. These are all set in the properties of each video you upload. Be sure to set three properties for every video you upload to maximize your visibility. A YouTube channel can be created for free on the YouTube website.

Like all social media, YouTube videos can be shared via other platforms such as Facebook and Twitter. So, make a note to share videos you upload to these channels through Facebook posts and tweets.

Instagram   Level of effort: Moderate   Value: Low

While less of a platform to present a carefully crafted message, Instagram can raise awareness of your school, create engagement with your community, and present a real and human face for your school. Instagram can be thought of as the visual equivalent of Twitter. Your Instagram account allows you to post your images to a feed that users can subscribe to. Like Twitter, users can find you images and your feed through searches that use hashtags like "#charterschool." While not a core part of your marketing effort, Instagram can be a fun and easy-to-use addition if you have students and faculty eager to submit photos.

Pinterest   Level of effort: Moderate   Value: Low

Similar to Instagram, Pinterest is essentially a photo-sharing site. Pinterest uses predefined categories for photos and does have a few defined for education. More focused on design, hobbies and consumer products, Pinterest provides an alternative to Instagram but is probably of marginal interest to school marketers. Consider Pinterest if you already have members of your faculty or staff who are active users; otherwise, your efforts could be better spent elsewhere.

Google+   Level of effort: High   Value: Moderate

The Google social media platform offers social media sharing and networks similar to Facebook but runs a distant second in reach and number of users. Most Google+ users will also be active Facebook users. While offering many of the same and some improved social sharing and networking features, you should start using Facebook as your primary platform and consider Google+ if you have the extra bandwidth to add and maintain a Google+ profile. In the coming years, Google+ may gain more traction and is worth keeping an eye on and pursuing if you have the resources.

Wikipedia: Level of effort: Low   Value: High

Creating a Wikipedia page is a simple one-time task that can lend a sense of history and credibility to your school or district and provide links back to your school's web presence and enhance your school's visibility in organic search results. Go to Wikipedia, create an account, and create an article for your school or district. Once you have created your article, you can simply leave it alone and only update it if there are important changes that merit an edit. Be sure to add your page to a watch list to allow you to get notifications of changes to your page. Wikipedia articles are subject to revision by the larger community of editors; so, you don't own the content the way you would for other social media account. Accordingly, you will want to set up the preferences for your Wikipedia account so that you will be notified if any changes are made.

PLANNING AND EXECUTION

With the number of social media channels and your audience's increased expectations for relevant and fresh content, it can be easy to become overwhelmed. Just as easily, you can start marketing initiatives through your website and social media that may quickly fall by the wayside and become abandoned relics of your once enthusiastic efforts.

With the shifts in technology and ease of use, planning has become more important than technical knowledge. With proper planning, you can pace your marketing efforts, distribute the effort in creating content, and create a unified voice and message.

Set Up a Team of Contributors

Find members of your administration and faculty who can be responsible for collecting and editing content for specific media channels. These team members may not be creating the content themselves, but they will act as resident experts on the kinds of content your school should be feeding into its Facebook page, Twitter feed, or YouTube channel. These team members can also be responsible for recruiting content from other members of your school's community. By assigning members particular areas of expertise and distributing the effort, you'll get higher-quality and more consistent content.

Set Goals

Set some reasonable goals for the kinds and frequency of content you want to post. Some minimum target goals might be as follows:

- One Facebook post per week
- One short blog post per month
- Three tweets per month
- One YouTube video every two months
- Three Instagram photos per month

With some manageable and measurable goals, you can distribute the effort among several contributors, and, then, the effort no longer seems so overwhelming. More than anything, set a pace that is sustainable.

Initially, you may want to seed your social media channels with some additional content to establish your presence and generate interest. However, what is most important is planning an effort that will allow your team to maintain a continually updated marketing presence at a sustainable pace.

TRANSLATE YOUR GOALS INTO A MARKETING CALENDAR AND FOLLOW IT

Take your goals and put them on a marketing calendar. Assign each marketing item to a team member and meet briefly biweekly or monthly to review completed and upcoming items and brainstorm on content ideas. A marketing calendar is the most important tool for establishing a consistent and constant social media presence that is sustainable for your contributors and easy to manage. The number one failure of technology marketing groups is starting initiatives, because they are easy and free, having an initial flurry of activity, and then abandoning the efforts for lack of content and interest. If you suddenly have five blog articles, ten ideas for Facebook posts, and three items to tweet, compose them as soon as you can, but put them on a calendar and stagger them out over weeks. Your team will be less stressed, more enthusiastic, and your pages and content will attract more traffic and consistent followers.

Social media will change as quickly as companies can create new products. Using the latest innovation is a constant learning process that requires some amount of enthusiasm, patience, and interest. The rewards can be great. Without some application of new technology the risk of losing ground in your marketing effort is real. If you are not using the channels that most people are using, your message is not going to be heard.

Companies are aware that the easier their products are to use, the more readily people will adopt them. So, even for those of us who are technology challenged will find these new innovations accessible. Remember much technology that seemed foreign and daunting at first has become routine and helpful.

Before you jump into blogs and tweets, know what you want to accomplish with social media. Look at the goals your team set for your marketing effort and see how you can use the new forms of communication to advance those goals. Include the person in charge of technology in your plans and implementation. You may want to try one medium before adding others. Visit other school or district sites to see what others are doing.

There is no doubt that the use of electronic communication can significantly improve two-way communication for schools and districts. Improving two-way communication is essential if schools and districts are to be responsive to their internal and external stakeholders. Like many initiatives, the greatest expenditure of time and money is in the beginning, but the long-term benefits are greater efficiency, better use of resources, and improved communication.

Chapter 2

Media Relations

It has been some time since a school's media experiences were mainly pictures in the local newspaper of a 4-H member proudly holding a blue ribbon with an arm around the prize-winning animal or a story about the choral group's holiday performance. Today, district administrators often view their dealings with the media with dread and suspicion.

In my experience, people who have children in public schools generally have a more favorable opinion of public education than people who do not. Because people without children in public schools generally have little or no contact with the school, they form their opinions through secondary sources, often the media. The astute administrator is one who recognizes the media's influence over public perception and makes an effort to work with the media rather than against it.

Most schools and school districts have a media, communication, or public affairs officer who is a professional with experience in interacting with the media. This chapter discusses ways in which school administrators can help their media relations or communication administrator maximize relations with the media by reducing occasions for negative media coverage within their own school environment and by working with neighborhood news services to create an awareness of the school's achievements and activities.

If your school or district is without a position dedicated to media relations, it is important that one administrator be named as the contact person for all news releases and media requests. Having multiple people speak for the school or district can lead to unnecessary confusion and misleading information. This chapter can assist those individuals to develop media relations that will benefit the school and keep the community informed.

GETTING THE NEWS OUT

Most people want to know what is going on in their local schools whether they have children in them or not. This is especially true when educational issues are gaining national attention. No one knows better what is going on in the schools than the administrators and staff members. Providing positive newsworthy items to the media office or to neighborhood papers can play a major role in improving community relations. The school can increase the chances of getting its story told by knowing what constitutes a "good" news item and how to make those items interesting.

There are two reasons why people read or listen to a news item. One is because it contains information they want or need to know. These "hard news" items provide information in a factual, objective, impersonal way. A story about progress on flood damage repairs to the school and how it will affect the beginning of the school year is a hard news story. When submitting this type of news item, provide the most important information, *who, what, when where, why,* and *how* in the first paragraph, then follow with greater detail in subsequent paragraphs. Check all factual material for accuracy, avoid using jargon, and be able to provide the source(s) of secondary information.

The factual, objective nature of the hard news story does not mean there is no opportunity to show the school in a positive light. In the above-mentioned example about flood damage repair, the news item could point out that processes put in place by the school administration resulted in the project being ahead of schedule or that the school has contingency plans in the event of unexpected delays.

Even a negative story can have positive effects if handled properly. A story about bus breakdowns causing children to be repeatedly late for school may give support to the school's or district's need to replace old buses.

A second reason people read or listen to news items is because they find them entertaining or interesting. The feature story provides information but in a more engaging, attention-grabbing way. Feature stories are an opportunity to create positive awareness of the school. Stories may be of interest because they link to something in the national news, involve an interesting person, describe the school's innovative approach to an issue, or announce an outstanding achievement.

However, the story has to be interesting enough for people to take the time to read or listen to it. How do you get the public interested in reading a news item about the sixth grader in your school who won a regional spelling bee? Well, a few years ago, a documentary film about spelling bees drew audiences to major theaters across the country. How? It told an emotional, dramatic human interest story. Your articles do not have to be award winning, but they should tell the reader a good story.

First, create a headline that will attract interest. A headline that reads "Could you spell homoeothermic?" is more attention grabbing than one that reads "Local 6th grader wins regional spelling bee."

Once you have the reader's attention with the headline, keep it by making the news item a dramatic story, adding interesting personal information and tying it to the interests of the reader. Write about the tension surrounding the spelling bee, provide some interesting information about the winning student, and mention how competition for the spelling bee improved the spelling and vocabulary skills of the school's sixth-grade students.

Include an interesting photograph that depicts the drama in the story. For example, the child's face when she realizes she has won or the emotion-filled scene backstage before the finals. The photograph may or may not be included with the story, but it has a better chance if it is interesting and pertinent.

Preferably, the person developing and writing news items for the school will be on the marketing team. If there is no one who has the flair for developing stories, appoint a staff member who likes to write, use students from high school English or journalism classes, find a volunteer who has media experience, or check the local college for a journalism student looking for part-time work. The person you select should be willing to make a commitment for the school year. It is also important that an administrator or the schools' or district's media relations person approve all news items that are submitted to any media outlet.

Both hard news and feature stories are opportunities to promote your school. Remember that the media are more likely to run a story if the item is well written and the content has audience appeal.

GET TO KNOW THE NEIGHBORHOOD NEWSPAPERS

If your school is located in a large city or town, there may be weekly papers that cover a specific section of the town or papers that are designed for a specific cultural group. These area papers are a good way to tell local residents about the events and accomplishments at your school.

Neighborhood papers are always looking for stories about what is happening in the area, and school news is interesting to many area residents. Generally, neighborhood papers are distributed free through local merchants so people often read them more frequently than major city papers. This makes them a good avenue for disseminating information and promoting school activities.

Personal relationships are important in media relations. Because these papers are small operations, it is easier to develop personal relationships with staff members. Building a relationship with the paper can generate a valuable level of trust that is beneficial to the school and the paper. Begin by setting up an introductory meeting between the paper's staff members and the person who will be working directly with the paper.

The school's principal should be more than just a name or title. Therefore, it is important that the principal be present at the introductory meeting even if he or she will not be the primary contact with the paper. The principal's presence conveys the importance the school places on the relationship and establishes a personal rapport.

Before the first meeting, look through several recent publications and read articles and editorials to learn something about the paper and its writers. During the meeting, ask about deadlines, preferences for story length, how articles and press releases should be formatted, photographic requirements, and special interests the paper may have. Follow up the meeting with a thank-you note. Put the paper on the school's mailing list. Invite the paper's staff members to visit the school and send them invitations to school events.

Once you have established a rapport with your local paper, take care to maintain it. Respect the guidelines that the paper has established, especially those related to deadlines. Do not expect the paper to print everything you submit; although if the stories are well written and timely, they probably will.

Get to know the local media that focus their programming or reporting on special ethnic populations within the community. Foreign-language newspapers and radio and television stations are outstanding sources for incoming and outgoing information. Because they are in the news business, print and broadcast media are especially aware of major issues in the community. Their language capabilities and credibility within the community make them excellent disseminators of news to specific groups within the school's environment. Ask reporters for their assistance in effective outreach to their listeners or readers.

If you are submitting articles to a paper that publishes in a language other than English, be sure that your article is accurately translated. If there is no one in your school who is fluent in the second language, ask a trusted member of the local community who is to assist you. If no one can assist you, require that your article be printed in English along with the translated article so content accuracy can be maintained. Keep the language in the article simple; do not use slang or unfamiliar terms that are difficult to translate.

MEDIA RELATIONS IS TWO-WAY

Remember, relationships are two way. This applies to the media as well. There are times—for example, at the beginning of the school year—when the media are looking for local school news. Be prepared to meet requests with useful information. By informing the media about educational matters, the school can help reporters better understand the legal, financial, and political issues that schools face and how those issues affect decisions. If there are national or state education matters that the paper wants to address, be available to discuss the issues with them. Try to anticipate what kinds of questions the reporter may want to ask and be prepared to answer them. Have supporting data or sources for any statistics or facts you provide. If the community is concerned about standardized testing, provide the reporter with background on the whys and wherefores of testing. Help the reporter develop a holistic view of an issue by providing differing opinions.

The media are in the news business. Do not expect them to overlook negative issues. If negative events involving the school occur, be available to answer questions. It is an opportunity for the school to get its side of the story told.

Always compliment a reporter on a well-crafted story. Thank them when the school's news stories or press releases are used. Conversely, if a reporter's story was unfair or distorted, convey your opinion respectfully, and, if warranted, write a letter to the editor or station manager to state the school's side.

UTILIZE YOUR DISTRICT COMMUNICATION OFFICE

Even though you may be regularly sending newsletters to the people in your neighborhood, important events and accomplishments should receive citywide attention. If your school is in a large district with cross enrollment or there are similar private or charter schools in your area, you may be competing for the same students. Getting positive publicity in citywide publications or major media news sources is a way to promote your school to prospective students outside the school's immediate community.

Do not wait for someone to notice your school. Put together your own stories and photographs in a form that meets the school's or district's requirements and submit them to the press or communication officer in a timely manner. Your school's news is more likely to make it into print if you create interesting articles that do not require a lot of reworking.

Be sure to contact your communication or press office immediately in the event of a crisis at the school. Provide as much information as possible. The media office is limited in its ability to help you if the information you provide is inaccurate or incomplete.

PRESS RELEASES

Press releases are a way to tell the community about the good things that are happening in the school. Just because you write a press release, however, does not mean the media will use it. Reporters are looking for *interesting* stories. Beyond being interesting, reporters want press releases that require a minimum of work on their part. If a reporter has to spend time making your story fit a specific format, she may not use it. A well-crafted press release will gain the respect of most reporters. Below are suggestions for writing a news release that is "fit to print":

- At the top of the press release provide the following information: name and address of school, time and date, school contact person with telephone number and e-mail address.
- Have a clear, concise headline that will draw interest.
- Double space the text.
- Include all the most important information in the first paragraph. Answer all the *Who, What, When, Where, How, and Why* questions. For example:

  Today *(when)* Riverside High School *(who)* announced a $200,000 grant *(what)* from XYZ Corporation *(who)* to expand its award-winning Tomorrow's Scientists Program *(why)*. Riverside High School will use the grant funds to upgrade its present laboratory facilities *(where)* and provide professional development opportunities for its dedicated science teachers *(how)*.

  This format ensures that if people do not read beyond the first paragraph, they have the most important information.
- Use remaining paragraphs to provide additional information.
- Stick with facts and avoid hyperbole. Provide support for key points, opinions, and claims.

- Do not editorialize. This is not an opinion piece.
- Use interesting and pertinent quotes.
- Do not use jargon.
- Keep it under two pages.
- Check for spelling and grammar errors.
- Submit the press release in a timely manner.

Do not be upset if the item is not used or if only part of it is used. Media staff members other than the reporter may make those decisions. Keep submitting items that you feel are newsworthy and interesting. If your press releases are consistently rejected, ask media representatives how to make them more acceptable.

USE KEY COMMUNICATORS IN THE COMMUNITY TO DISPEL UNFAIR PRESS COVERAGE

One of the best ways to mitigate the effects of negative news stories is to maintain a positive impression of the school through the school's key communicators. Think of a time when someone attacked the character of a person you knew and held in high regard. Did you simply accept the negative assertions and think less of your acquaintance? Likely, you defended your acquaintance and challenged the accuser's statements.

Key communicators touch many people in the community through their business and civic activities. If the media have misrepresented the facts in a story about the school or district, act swiftly to inform your key communicators of the specific inaccuracies and provide them with the correct details. If they hear negative stories repeated, they will then have the information to correct them.

Particularly egregious misrepresentations may require that the school or district hold a press conference to state its case. In such an event, having key communicators publicize and attend the news conference shows community support.

CRISIS SITUATIONS REQUIRE A PLAN

Few administrators would view handling a crisis as a marketing opportunity, but having a procedure in place that allows the school to deal with any potential crisis effectively and efficiently should be part of your marketing plan. In part, the community judges the school by its preparedness for and its response to a crisis. How you handle a crisis is a measure of a school's concern for its students, employees, and the community at large. Mismanagement of a crisis can undo the goodwill and support that the school has worked so hard to build.

In a crisis, the community and the media want information. In addition, parents and staff members want assurance that the school is in control of those things it can control and is doing what it can to address the crisis. How the school handles the situation in the first few minutes and hours is critical. These are moments when high emotions create strong and lasting perceptions, whether justified or not.

The majority of good crisis management takes place before a crisis happens. Having a plan in which everyone understands his or her role will mitigate the chaos that exacerbates a crisis. A school crisis manager and crisis management team, including school counselors, security personnel, and those in charge of school communication, should establish contingency plans. The team should also be responsible for implementing the plan in the event of a crisis. Select individuals you can depend upon to be responsible, rational, and calm under stress.

The team cannot predict every crisis, but it can anticipate those that are likely to occur in a school environment, such as violence; drugs; bus accidents; administrator, staff member, or teacher misconduct; fires; weather disasters; medical emergencies; and financial or compliance irregularities.

Issues considered in creating crisis plans should include the following:

- What crises might occur and what specific actions should the school take in each case?
- What district-wide policies and procedures should be incorporated into the school plan?
- What emergency assistance agencies should the school contact? What specific information should the school provide to them?
- Who out of people such as clergy, psychologists, law enforcement liaisons, hazardous material specialists, and others can the school call upon to provide pre- and postcrisis guidance and counseling?
- Who will be the primary source of information to the central administration, staff members, students, parents, and media? What information should the school provide to these groups?
- What channels of communication are available to the school and how can we best use them?
- What translation capabilities are available for community communications?

- Are there sufficient key people, such as coaches, nurses, and teachers, trained in CPR?
- What training and materials are available to ensure that *all* employees are knowledgeable about crisis procedures?
- What are the legal issues concerning liability and confidentiality?
- Do front office staff members, who may receive telephone threats, have proper training?
- What lessons have been learned from past experiences?
- What can we learn from other schools' or districts' experiences?
- What information is available from external agencies and groups that we can use?

In answering these questions, the planning group should be able to gather enough information to create procedure manuals and develop scenario planning. At least once a year the group should meet to review plans and make required changes.

EFFECTIVE CRISIS COMMUNICATION IS CRITICAL

Effective communication is critical when a crisis occurs. Rumors and unsubstantiated reports can exacerbate the crisis and foster panic. Getting information to internal and external groups is a key element in crisis control.

It is the responsibility of the district or school to communicate quickly, completely, and honestly with all internal and external groups. The best way to be prepared is to have a crisis communication plan. The goal is to aim for containment of the situation, not suppression of information.

The superintendent, dean, communication officer, or principal may be designated as the key spokesperson for the school or district. In addition to the designated spokesperson, there should be a backup person. Both these people should be well versed in handling a crisis.

Advise staff members and students not to give out information to the media, but to refer them to the key spokesperson. Of course, the reality is that in the middle of a crisis and in the immediate aftermath, the media will try to get information from anyone they can whether or not the source is official or reliable. Nevertheless, it is important to remind staff members and students in crisis procedure training and communication materials of the importance of leaving communication to the appropriate person.

The school's key community communicators can help the school disseminate information. It is advisable to include these individuals in creating your communication plan. At the least, they should be aware of what your plan is.

Telephone numbers of parents and guardians should be easily accessible and in multiple forms. An information database housed on a computer system is not accessible if power is lost or the system goes down. Have backup capabilities. Those responsible for calling parents should not engage in long conversations or speculation with them. Use the time only to inform parents of what has happened and what the school is doing. Have people available to communicate with non-English-speaking parents. An emergency information site on the school website can help get information out quickly. The community should be made aware of this information site. Many schools now have automated call systems that can be activated in the case of an emergency.

Students should hear crisis information from someone they trust. A person trained to deal with various reactions should be present. Give students a place to go. Do not leave them alone. An appropriate person should be available if students want to talk.

Telephone numbers and names of contact persons within the media and other organizations should also be readily available. The key spokesperson should be available to provide to the media some details in response to the following questions:

- What has happened?
- Who was involved?
- Was anyone killed or injured? Details such as names are not necessary and in most cases *should not* be provided until information is verified and necessary persons notified. Names of minors should not be released.
- Where did it happen?
- When did it happen?
- How did it happen?
- What is currently being done?

In dealing with the media, the following suggestions will help the spokesperson stay in control of the interview:

- Get the important facts out first.
- Do not speculate or give opinions when answering questions.
- If you do not know something, say so.
- Tell the truth.
- Do not argue with the reporter.
- Remember, nothing is off the record.
- Do not let reporters define the crisis. Correct any misinformation or misinterpretation of information immediately.
- Promptly provide promised follow-up information.

As information comes in, disseminate it to the appropriate people. If possible, someone should document what has happened, what is being done, who has been contacted, and any other useful information that the administration can use at the time or later to assess the situation.

GIVING AN INTERVIEW

Generally, the school's or district's communication or press officer deals with the media. However, in some circumstances, it is advantageous for the principal or other administrator to grant an interview. If the school has garnered an outstanding award or has had success with one of its programs, certainly an interview is a good way to communicate that news to the public. However, in circumstances where the news is not good, an interview is a way to neutralize bad press or to show that the school has nothing to hide. If you are scheduled for an interview, here are some tips to consider:

- Be prepared. Know what you want to say and be prepared to say it in a concise and understandable way. Try to anticipate the kinds of questions the interviewer will ask and have the information to back up your answers. You do not have to commit all facts and figures to memory. When the information is particularly complex, it is acceptable to say, "I am referring to data I have compiled by federal agencies which show . . ." or "I have here copies of inspection reports which show . . ." Use mock interviews to practice, preferably with someone like the district communications officer who has experience with the interview process. Make mock interviews as realistic as possible with tough questions, prolonged silences, and aggressive follow-ups from the interviewer. Tape the mock interview and then critique it. Look for gestures, posture, eye movements, repetitive phrases, annoying "fillers," and facial expressions that may produce a negative response. Tape the actual interview. Having your own audio- or videotape of the interview allows you to rectify any statements taken out of context, misquotes, or inaccuracies. Knowing that a tape of the interview exists may also dissuade the interviewer from putting an inappropriate slant on the final product.
- Follow the press release format for your main message. Be brief, but get your message across. Begin by giving the most important information first, then elaborating. Otherwise, you may not be able to get in the points that you want to make. Do not use jargon or language that makes you sound condescending. Speak in a way that will appeal to those listening to or reading the interview. Do not exaggerate or use excessive adjectives for effect.

"We are proud of our students" is a more powerful statement than "We are actually really very proud of our students."

- Do not let the interviewer put words in your mouth. If an interviewer describes the latest test scores as disastrous, you do not have to accept his assessment. Repeating his assessment by saying "Our scores were not disastrous" only reinforces the statement. Instead, say, "On the contrary, our scores exceeded all schools in the district accept one. Scores for most schools were lower this year because of the new testing requirements."
- Beware of the deadly silence. Sometimes an interviewer will not respond to an answer or simply become silent hoping that the interviewee will become flustered and attempt to fill in the void (with some thoughtless remark). If you have said all that you want to say and the interviewer just looks at you, remain calm and wait for the next question.
- Be truthful, be honest, and do not lie. Do not be tempted to distort the truth even a little bit. Speak the truth even if it hurts. Have you heard the saying, "The cover-up can be worse than the crime"? How many business leaders, politicians, even clergy have made situations worse and prolonged the media's scrutiny by lying. If the media catch someone in a lie, it provides justification for additional and more intense investigation. Generally, people are understanding and even forgiving, unless you lie to them.
- Dress appropriately. If you are being interviewed for television, wear conservative clothing in subdued colors. Avoid large patterns and plaids, especially in bright colors. A cream-colored blouse or shirt looks better on camera than a stark white one. A bit of color in a tie or scarf will prevent you from looking too somber.
- Do not argue or become emotional. No matter how much the interviewer baits or attacks you, try to remain calm. As with the use of silence, the interviewer hopes that you will become provoked and blurt out an emotional statement. Do not argue. It will make the situation worse. If you do not know the answer to a question, say so and offer to get the information the interviewer wants.
- Remember, nothing is off the record. Even if you consider the interviewer a friend, nothing is off the record. Reporters' success depends on getting a story. Few reporters will walk away from a good story because someone said, "Now, this is just between you and me, right?"
- Do not be lulled into a false sense of security by a smiling reporter who is asking you warm and fuzzy questions. The next question may be a hard-hitting question that takes you by surprise. The best approach is to have a message and stay on the message.

Dealing with the media should not and need not be a negative situation. Most reporters are not out to get you, but they are responsible for getting as much information as possible about a specific issue. Look upon the media as an avenue for informing the public about the positive aspects of your school or district. Do your part to help reporters do a better job of informing the public. Be prepared for crisis situations. Be honest, informative, and available when events go wrong. If treated unfairly by the media, take measures to disseminate the truth and dissuade future misrepresentation.

Chapter 3

Building Community Partnerships

In the past, schools' requests for support from external groups were limited to the occasional need for door prizes, sponsorship of events, and raising money for special student trips. Today, greater demands combined with fewer resources require that schools look to external sources for more and different kinds of support. Schools are entering into more defined, long-term partnerships with external partners than in the past.

School administrators recognize that building stronger community relationships can provide much needed resources. Yet every year districts and schools lose thousands, even hundreds of thousands, of dollars in goods and services and immeasurable amounts of goodwill from the businesses and organizations in their communities. How? My interviews with businesses and organizations indicate that some of the most common reasons why they choose not to work with a school or district are the following:

- Lack of accountability for goods or services received
- Lack of planning
- Lack of professional courtesy
- Lack of follow through
- Lack of appreciation

This chapter provides suggestions for addressing these obstacles to better partnerships.

Businesses and organizations can help in a number of ways: mentoring, class speakers, student internships, scholarships, event sponsorship, workplace tours, staff development, and providing goods and services. In return, schools can give their partners positive publicity by acknowledging their contributions in several ways: announcements on the school's marquee, articles in the school newsletter and website, signs or posters that businesses can display, banners, and media coverage of partnership events and programs. Public awareness benefits both sides of the partnership. The business or organization is recognized as a contributing member of the community and the school is recognized as having community support.

WHAT MAKES A GOOD PARTNERSHIP?

A partnership is a continuous, mutually beneficial relationship between the school and an external organization. The key words here are *continuous* and *mutually beneficial.*

Have you ever had an acquaintance whom you heard from only when he wanted something? After a while, you dreaded his calls. Businesses often report that the only time they hear from schools is when they need something. The school can foster a positive relationship with its partners by keeping in contact through newsletters, notes from the students, teachers, and staff members, invitations to school events and meetings, annual reports, and partner appreciation activities.

In one of my workshops, a school administrator complained that a local grocery store that had helped the school in the past was not returning her phone calls. What should she do? Further questioning revealed that the last time the school had any contact with the store was 18 months earlier when the store had helped the school with a project. No one from the school had bothered to keep in contact. I suggested she try to rebuild the relationship through interaction that offered a benefit to the store or its employees such as "Partnership Recognition Night" at a school sporting event, tickets to a school sporting event or play for the store employees, or inclusion of the store manager in a community leadership breakfast. After the relationship is reestablished, the school can work with the store in mutually beneficial projects. Companies will be more receptive to school requests if they keep in touch.

Many businesses and organizations are eager and willing to help schools, but they expect something in return, even if it is only confirmation that what they are doing is truly helping the students. Therefore, it is crucial that these relationships be *quid pro quo*, an equal exchange, something for something. If the business sees the school only as an extended empty hand waiting to be filled, the relationship eventually will be unrewarding for both sides.

When schools enter into a partnership with an organization, they should be aware of what the partner expects and how they can meet those expectations.

It is not the responsibility of the school's partners to assess the school's needs and determine how to meet them. Businesses report that they are willing to help schools with their needs, but the schools should come to them with an understanding of what the needs are, a strategy to address those needs, and specific ideas for how their partners can help and benefit.

Every marketing effort should have goals and an honest assessment of what activities and resources are required to achieve those goals. To establish a needs assessment, ask the following:

- What goals came out of the school's assessment?
- What resources does the school need to reach those goals?
- Are there groups in the community that can help the school achieve those goals? How?
- Who are the school's past, present, and potential partners?
- What is the school's present relationship with external organizations?
- What can the school do for its partners?

The school marketing team, with input from staff members, should assess what the school's needs are, then rank them. Start with the top two or three and rewrite them as project goals. Next, construct plans for meeting each goal, determine how partners can help, and list the benefits to both the school and the partners. You may need a plan to meet each goal.

Write the plan in the form of a clear and concise proposal that you can present to your partners (see an example in the case study found in this chapter). Provide support materials to clarify the goal and to describe how the school will use the contributions to attain it. For example, a plan to improve the school's landscaping might include a photograph of the schoolyard as it presently is with an explanation of the improvements the school hopes to make. Any written items submitted to partners, such as proposals and support materials, must be professional in appearance and content.

The school has the responsibility to maximize the benefits of contributions to the school, the students, and the contributors. The team should also consider the school's ability to manage increased support. A school may receive funds, equipment, materials, or services only to find that the staff members or students are incapable or unwilling to utilize the contribution. Companies report that employees have volunteered to mentor students only to find that the school was too disorganized to take advantage of the contribution, or that a school did not have the internal capabilities to implement a plan, thereby wasting monetary contributions.

After the evaluation is complete, divide the potential partners in your community into three action categories: Reaffirm–Reconnect–Reach Out.

REAFFIRMING PRESENT PARTNERSHIPS

If partnerships already exist, the school should take action to enhance those relationships. Create a profile for each partner (see an example in the case study found in this chapter). The profile will help the school cultivate the relationship. Each partner profile provides a history of the relationship that will survive staff changes, help to customize communication, and match school requests to the partners' interests and capabilities.

Create a database of all partners or include them in your present database with an indicator that they are partners. At a minimum, the database should include names and titles, phone and fax numbers, and addresses of all contact persons. A database will allow quick retrieval of all contact information. Utilize the database for newsletters, invitations, school announcements, e-mails, social media, and meeting reminders. Use the Internet to search for recent positive news articles about partners and send a brief note to acknowledge the good press coverage. If changes in contact people occur, send the new person information on the school and invite her to visit the school.

Develop a tracking form for partner contributions (see an example in the case study found in this chapter). The tracking form establishes a history that allows the school to provide the partner with an annual report of contributions.

RECONNECTING WITH PAST PARTNERS

Valuable relationships may have ended because the external organizations found no benefit to the partnerships, or they may have withered away from lack of attention. In some cases, economic downturns or turnover within a company causes it to focus on other priorities.

Assess the status and history of the school with the partners. Here is an instance when having a partner profile and contribution tracking system would provide valuable information. Determine why the relationship is not active and what the school can do to rebuild it.

It may require some effort to find out why the partner is no longer involved with the school. Company representatives may be reluctant to justify why the relationship has deteriorated. The usual excuse is that, "Things have changed in the organization" or "We are reassessing our priorities." If you have a good rapport with people in the company who worked with the school, ask them for an honest assessment of what went wrong. Be prepared that in extreme cases it may take time or a change in the company's management before they are willing to resume the partnership.

If it looks as though the school can reestablish the partnership, reconnect with a note, letter, or invitation (see an example in the case study found in this chapter). Do not reconnect by asking for something.

REACHING OUT TO POTENTIAL PARTNERS

New businesses or organizations may have moved into the area, and some established businesses may never have been contacted. Research by the marketing team can identify potential partners within the businesses and organizations in the community. List the identified groups and put those with the highest perceived potential at the top of your list. Then take steps to reach out to these groups. Start with the top five in your list.

Do not expect potential partners to come to the school. Although some national and regional companies have established programs for working with schools, many more do not. Many businesses report that they would be open to working with a local school if a school administrator contacted them in a professional and organized way. Some businesses simply never thought about it. Few companies, however, are willing to spend time trying to determine what a school needs and how to help. That is the school's job.

Find out who in the organization is the best contact person. Most medium to large companies have a public relations or community relations person who handles external relationships. Ask current partners, parents, or community leaders if they are acquainted with any of the potential partners and would be willing to make introductions, provide referrals for you, or supply information about individuals or the business that can make your initial contact more personal.

Send out an introduction letter to businesses and organizations (see an example in the case study found in this chapter). The letter should be an introduction only. The purpose is to start building a rapport. Follow up with a telephone call or, if possible, a brief visit. If an event is occurring at the school, include an invitation.

If the business or organization is new to the area, send a welcome letter *(see an example in the case study found in this chapter).*

Create a partnership interest survey *(see an example in the case study found in this chapter)* and send it to businesses that have responded in some way to the school's initial letter. The survey should not be an appeal for contributions but rather a sincere request for information. Use the information to begin a partner profile. Include the organizations in the school's database and begin sending them your mail-outs.

MAKING YOUR FIRST MEETING A SUCCESS

Your initial meeting sets the tone of the relationship. Here are a few guidelines to help make your initial meeting a success:

- Find out who the contact person is and make an appointment.
- Before the meeting, find out something about the business or organization from the company's website. As you look at the website, ask these questions:
  - What does the company or organization do?
  - How long has the business or organization been in the area?
  - Who are the key people?
  - Have they participated in community or philanthropic activities?
  - What is the organization's philosophy (usually contained in their mission or vision statement or in their advertisements)?
  - Have there been any interesting, positive news stories about the company (usually contained in their "media or press articles" page)?
- Call the day before to confirm the meeting and be prepared to reschedule if necessary.
- Be on time for the meeting. Arriving late for meetings is a common complaint from businesses.
- Dress professionally.
- If the organization had a partnership with the school in the past, try to find out as much as you can about the past relationship. Be prepared to address any negative aspects of past partnerships.
- Offer a packet of information about the school. Include in the packet information about present partnerships, copies of any newspaper articles related to partnerships, photographs of partnership activities with the school, and a summary of partnership activities.
- Think about the school's goals. How do they align with those of the potential partner? Is there a mutual interest in science, the arts, literacy, the

environment, or sports? Consider ways the school can support the partner's interests.

- Do not ask for anything in the initial meeting. The purpose is to introduce yourself and the school and to begin a relationship.
- Invite the person to visit the school or to participate in a partnership breakfast or event.
- Keep the meeting short.
- Send a thank-you note after the meeting.
- Put the organization on the school's mailing list and keep in touch.

YOUR PARTNERS DESERVE ACCOUNTABILITY

Businesses are result oriented. To justify initiating or continuing contributions, businesses need to know that their efforts are producing positive results. One of the principal complaints from businesspeople is that often they have no idea whether what they are doing is really helping the students. If a company is allowing employees to volunteer hours in the school, they want to know how the volunteers are helping the students. If the school received a monetary contribution, the organization wants to know how the funds were spent and what benefits were provided. To let partners know how their contributions benefit the students and the school, give them an annual report with clear examples.

The school's ability to provide documentation of contributions may determine whether a company enters into a partnership. Companies may be required to provide documentation of their support to their corporate office. If the company must spend time gathering and compiling documentation material, they may be reluctant to become involved. In some instances, documentation is necessary for tax purposes. Ask your partner in the beginning what level of documentation the company needs.

TIME IS MONEY

In the private sector, the often-repeated saying "Time is money" is true. When businesspeople set aside time to meet with school representatives, they are donating the dollars attached to employee productivity and time.

Missing appointments, chronic tardiness, not returning phone calls promptly, or indifference from the school's administration and staff members indicate a lack of appreciation for your partners' time and money. Businesses report taking employees away from their duties for a meeting with a school representative who did not come and did not call. Company employees report showing up for volunteer work only to find that the class had gone on a field trip. This is a waste of the partner's time and money.

It is the responsibility of all school personnel to keep appointments and to be on time. The same rules apply to communication. Your business partners are too busy to call you for no reason; if they call, there is a reason. Administrators should respond to calls and e-mails promptly. Teachers and office staff members should be prepared for volunteers and have meaningful work for them to do.

CAN YOU MAKE A COMMITMENT?

People enter into relationships with certain expectations of the each other. Continued inability or unwillingness to meet those expectations by one side will result in reluctance to continue by the other. Businesses and organizations generally want confirmation that their contributions are helping the students, that they will receive positive recognition, and that their efforts will enhance their image in the community.

It is tempting to make promises when the school is eager to get a project going. Those promises must be kept. Before entering into a partnership, the school should have an understanding of the external organization's expectations, the school's ability to meet those expectations, and a commitment to follow through.

Likewise, schools have expectations of what their partners will do and make plans accordingly. Schools should feel confident that their partners will provide the promised support.

The best way to eliminate misunderstandings that come from ambiguity is to write expectations for both sides in a partnership agreement like the example below. Putting the school's and the partner's expectations in writing encourages each side to consider what will be required to follow through on their commitments.

LINCOLN MIDDLE SCHOOL

Partnership Agreement

This agreement is entered into by and between Lincoln Middle School located at 3478 Elm Street, Houston, Texas 77019 and [Name of Partner], located at

(Address of Partner) for the purpose of enhancing the educational experience of the students at Lincoln Middle School.

(Name of Partner) agrees to abide by the policies and procedures of the district.

WHEREAS Lincoln Middle School seeks to provide the best possible learning environment for its students through collaborative efforts with community partners, and

WHEREAS (Name of Partner) desires to assist Lincoln Middle School in that effort.

Lincoln Middle School and (Name of Partner) now enter into an agreement in which (Name of Partner) agrees to the following:

(Here, list the contribution(s) agreed upon by the organization. Example: XYZ Computer Store will allow any of our technology employees to donate a maximum of ½ day each semester for the purpose of improving Lincoln Middle School students' computer skills.)

And, Lincoln Middle School agrees to the following:

(Here, list activities agreed upon by school. Example: Lincoln Middle School will list XYZ Computer Store as a PAL Patron in all school newsletters, on the school website, on our school posters, and in our annual report. The school will also create awareness of support activities by XYZ Corporation through social media such as the school's webpage, Facebook page, and Twitter account.)

This partnership shall begin on (Date) and be terminated by either party with 14 days notice.

_____

(Signature for Lincoln Middle School)   (Signature for Partner)

NEVER STOP SAYING "THANK YOU"

People like to be appreciated. Companies are made up of people. Do not lapse into thinking of companies, organizations, or even groups of people as impersonal entities. There are other schools in your community who will appreciate your partners if you do not.

The school can say "thank you" in many ways.

- Notes and letters from the school, especially from the students
- A message on the school marquee

- An article in the local paper
- An article in the school newsletter
- Nomination of partners for local or national awards
- A recognition luncheon
- A "thank you" on the school website
- Invitations to school events
- A partnerships page in the annual report
- A banner at school events
- An hour of holiday music at noon in the partner's office lobby
- A large poster that can be displayed in the partner's place of business recognizing its contributions
- A Partnership Wall at the school (include photographs of events, outings, volunteers)
- An Appreciation Rally in which teachers and students verbally express thanks to company representatives through speeches, skits, music, or dance
- A Partner Recognition Week when students create posters and artwork or write stories; arrange the students' work in a display that celebrates the efforts of business partners, and then give it to the company to exhibit in the company's offices

Just keeping in touch with partners is a way to let them know that the school appreciates them. Do not forget the people who are volunteering their time. Send birthday cards or end-of-year thank-you notes to volunteers and mentors. Provide them with feedback on their contributions. Company employees often must use personal time to volunteer. If someone donates one hour to the school, she must come an hour earlier, leave an hour later, or use her lunchtime. That kind of dedication deserves to have affirmation of the school's appreciation. A company manager I interviewed for this book had two pieces of artwork, which he had framed, on his office wall. They were made and sent to him by two students he had mentored as a volunteer. He said it was that kind of appreciation that kept him volunteering.

In addition to personal expressions of appreciation from the teachers and students to volunteers, send a note to the contact person at the volunteer's company. Unless the thank-you letter or note is a follow-up to a major project with numerous participants, do not send form thank-you letters. Personally, I find a form thank-you letter or note almost as bad as none at all. The volunteer may have given hours of his time; fifteen minutes to write a note is not too much to ask. Below is an example of a brief but personalized way to recognize the contribution of a volunteer's time:

Ms. Marianne Wilson
Director of Community Relations
Citizen's Bank
123 Main Street
Houston, Texas 77077

Dear Marianne,

We truly enjoyed the opportunity to have Mr. Chen speak to the 6th grade about the Chinese New Year. The children enjoyed seeing his photographic slides and they were delighted by the authentic dragon costume. After Mr. Chen's presentation, many of the children expressed an interest in learning more about China. Some of the students have chosen to write class reports on Chinese architecture and the Great Wall of China. The students and I thank Citizen's Bank for sharing Mr. Chen with us.

Sincerely,
Hal Crockett
Teacher, 6th Grade Social Studies
Lincoln Middle School

Administrators should attend district-sponsored events that acknowledge the contributions of external partners. A school district recently lamented to me that it had gone to considerable effort and expense to host an appreciation luncheon for businesses that had supported the district and its schools throughout the year. Of the 34 schools that had benefited from this support, only 8 of the principals came to the luncheon. The others were "too busy." If school administrators cannot give up two hours at lunch to recognize the many hours of labor and thousands of dollars of support, then they should not be surprised when companies move their contributions elsewhere.

MAKING YOUR PARTNERS FEEL SPECIAL

A sponsor logo is special way to recognize your school's partners. Adapt the present school logo to create a special partnership logo or design an original one specifically for partnerships.

Businesses or organizations can display the partner logo on decals and posters in their place of business or in their advertisements to show their support for your school. Parents can be encouraged to patronize businesses that display the logo.

Use the logo on all communication regarding partnerships and include it in annual reports and newsletters, on banners, Facebook page, event programs, and the school marquee—wherever partners are recognized for their contributions. Be sure to follow all copyright requirements when designing logos from purchased clip art.

DO NOT PREJUDGE

"We don't have any businesses in our area." I hear this statement frequently from schools. Generally, what they mean is that the school does not have a *large* business or organization that could become their single benefactor. Schools often ignore small businesses and civic organizations in the community that can make small, but significant contributions. Following are potential partners that exist within most communities:

Branch banks
Car dealerships
Medical and dental clinics
Libraries
Neighborhood newspapers
Copy centers and printers
Restaurants
Shopping centers
Fitness centers
Major chain stores
Grocery stores
Family-owned businesses
Professional firms (high-tech, architectural, legal)
Organizations (civic clubs, garden clubs, nonprofit organizations)

These groups can contribute in many ways large and small. A copy center can help with the newsletter. A bank or library can host school exhibits. A fitness center may donate a three-month trial membership as a door prize. Businesses can put up posters for school events or help with fund-raising projects. A restaurant can provide food for meetings or an appreciation luncheon.

Build relationships with civic leaders in your community. Regular meetings with community leaders indicate the school's willingness to be an active member in promoting the entire community, not just your school. Include leaders from minority groups in your community.

Meetings with civic leaders, whether as group or one-on-one, are an excellent way to gather information that can help the school be proactive. If your school has meeting rooms, you could make them available to civic groups for meetings after-school hours. Display recent student projects and accomplishments for the groups to see.

Developing relationships with the external groups in the community is no longer becoming an optional activity for districts and schools. Building and maintaining these relationships should be a part of the marketing team's strategy.

Administrators should remember that businesses and organizations are not obligated to work with their schools (or any school). The number of organizations and the amount of assistance they can give are finite. Other schools and districts that are willing to work hard to acquire and keep partners may be competing for the same finite resources your school is.

Building partnerships requires a multifaceted approach. The following case study of Lincoln Middle School illustrates some of the ways to reaffirm, reconnect, and reach out to businesses and organizations in your community.

A CASE STUDY

LINCOLN MIDDLE SCHOOL

Lincoln Middle School has been in the community for over 15 years. Three months ago, Jim Hogan, who had been the principal for nine years, moved to another school, and his assistant principal, Amelia Flores, became the new principal. Amelia realizes that many of the changes she would like to make at the school are beyond the school's present resources. Moreover, Amelia recognizes the importance of good community relationships in supporting school initiatives such as attracting students, improving employee morale, and recruiting quality teachers.

Amelia recently formed a marketing team. A goal of the team is to build mutually beneficial partnerships with the businesses and organizations in the community. To move toward this goal, Amelia has appointed her assistant principal, Roland Carter, to serve as the coordinator of all partnership activities. Roland is also a member of the marketing team.

Amelia and Roland call their partnership initiative "The 3 Rs—Reaffirm, Reconnect, and Reach Out." Roland created an association for partners called Lincoln Middle School PAL (Partners Allied for Learning). PAL is open to all community businesses and organizations. A subgroup within PAL is PAL Patrons. PAL Patrons are organizations that have donated goods and services to Lincoln Middle School. The school recognizes their support in school communication pieces and other promotional activities. Roland has begun to schedule a monthly breakfast for all PAL members as a way to develop and maintain the partnerships by fostering continuing two-way communication.

To assist Roland in his efforts, the marketing team began by assessing their current partnerships. Lincoln Middle School has two ongoing partnerships that qualify as PAL Patrons. One is a software development company, SeismaTech, and one is a realty company, Reliance Realty. A few other businesses have helped with various needs in the past, but there has been little or no communication with them in a year.

To nurture their present partnerships, Amelia and Roland want the kind of data that is vital to maintaining good relationships. The marketing team has put present PAL members into a database and created a profile for each PAL Patron.

Below is a sample of a profile Roland created for SeismaTech. At the top, the profile provides contact information, a brief description of SeismaTech and the length of its partnership with Lincoln Middle School as a quick reference. But it is the specific details about interests, contributions, reciprocal activities, requirements, and comments contained in the profile that make it particularly valuable to nurturing this partnership.

The school gathers in-depth information of this kind through interaction with SeismaTech. Comments made during an event or meeting, appreciation expressed for a specific action, or specific requirements formally stated in an agreement are noted in the profile.

In this example, comments regarding how much the company president appreciates receiving thank-you notes from the children were noted in the profile. Roland uses this information to ensure that notes from the children are a follow-up activity to SeismaTech's contributions. Notation of formal requirements for proposals ensures compliance with company standards.

LINCOLN MIDDLE SCHOOL PAL PROFILE

Name of company or organization: SeismaTech, Inc.

Address:	123 Elm Street
	Houston, Texas 77019
	P.O. Box 12345
	Houston, Texas 77019-2345
Telephone	713.999.9999
Fax	713.999.9999

Contact Person:
Ms. Kathryn Simpson, Director of Public Relations

Other key people:
Ms. Lynn Jefferson, President
Mr. Steve Brown, Vice President of Marketing

Type of business or organization: Software development firm specializing in products for oil and gas exploration companies

Number of employees: 50

Year partnership initiated: 2010

Special interests:

The company president, Ms. Jefferson, is particularly interested in programs that encourage girls to consider high-tech careers. Ms. Jefferson is also an avid hiker and nature lover. She feels that children should participate more in outdoor activities especially those that involve enjoying and protecting nature.

Company's past and present activities or contributions:

In 2010, SeismaTech began a tutoring program. The company requests, but does not require, that each employee donate a minimum of 1/2 day each semester to help students improve computer skills. Since 2012, the company has sponsored an annual 1/2 day outing at the city's arboretum (transportation, picnic lunch, t-shirt, and a book on nature for each child) for the sixth grade science classes.

School's reciprocal activities:

Lincoln MS acknowledges SeismaTech's contributions on its marquee, its Facebook page, its website, and in the school newsletter. We also receive media coverage of our annual arboretum outing in neighborhood newspapers. SeismaTech is listed in our brochure and on our website as one of Lincoln Middle School's PAL Patrons.

Formal requirements:

All requests for contributions must be submitted via written proposals to the Director of Public Relations. All proposals must clearly define the expected benefits to the students.

Send Ms. Simpson a brief annual report on the number of hours donated by employees and the benefit to the children.

Comments:

Always send thank you notes from the children for the Arboretum Day. Ms. Simpson has commented on how much Ms. Jefferson appreciates hearing from the children. We always send invitations to school events to SeismaTech employees.

Profiles provide continuity and consistency. If the administration or composition of the marketing team changes, the profile provides new individuals with the information they need for continued success. You cannot rely on people's ability to remember or pass on essential information. I strongly recommend a profile for every school partner. Few schools have so many partners that creating and maintaining profiles would be a labor-intensive task. Once a profile is set up, it needs only occasional updating. The benefits far outweigh the effort.

Amelia and Roland want to reconnect with past partners. A past supporter of Lincoln Middle School is American Bank. At one time, the bank was a key supporter of the school; however, the school has had no contact with the bank for over a year. Roland heard from present PAL members that recently the bank underwent some organizational changes and several key people are new. Amelia suggests that Roland find out who the key contact is and send the person an invitation to the next PAL breakfast.

Your very first contact with a business or organization should be to get the correct information for your mailing list. You want the name of the person who would be most likely to interact with the school. If it is a small company or organization, the appropriate person is often the owner or president. Larger companies may have a person appointed to handle public or community relations. Get the correct spelling of the person's name, the position title, and a mailing address. If possible, get the name of the person's assistant.

This is not the time to ask for something. The purpose is just to get information for future communication. The conversation should be short.

In the first telephone contact, identify yourself and state your purpose to facilitate getting to the right person: "I am Roland Carter, the assistant principal of Lincoln Middle school, and I would like to get the name of the person in charge of community relations so I can send some information about our school's PAL program." People in businesses are more likely to help you if you state who you are and why you are calling. It conveys confidence that your call has merit.

Since many executives do not take calls from people whom they do not know, don't worry if you cannot speak with the person. You can get the information you need from the person's assistant.

It is wise to remember that secretaries and administrative assistants are the gatekeepers to executives. They are important people to know. I am constantly amazed at the lack of respect some people show for the work of office professionals. If a partnership develops between your school and the company, your contact person's assistant will be a key player in getting things done. Note the names of employees. When you call in the future, you can call people by name. It will create a positive and lasting impression. This may seem like an insignificant gesture; it is not.

I would like to make a comment here about addressing people. Although we live in a culture where most people operate on a first-name basis, do not assume that use of a person's first name is correct in all situations. Unless you live in a town or community where everyone knows everyone and uses first names of address, do not take for granted that it is welcome. Using casual forms of address too soon may offend some people. This is often the case with executives from foreign countries. Begin by using formal terms of address. If the relationship progresses, informal terms of address likely will be used; but, do not assume it is correct to do so in the beginning.

Be sure that you have the correct spelling of names and the correct titles. Not knowing how to spell someone's name is excusable, not finding out the correct spelling is not.

At the end of the call, thank the person who has helped you by name and state any immediate future actions, such as, "I will send Ms. Jennings an invitation to our business breakfast next week." These closing remarks may help the assistant recognize the invitation when it crosses her/his desk.

Using guidelines for effective communication, the Lincoln Middle School marketing team works on drafting the Reconnect and Reach Out letters to send to organizations from the list they have compiled. Roland asks Amelia to attach her name to all the initial letters. He knows that it is important for Amelia to take this opportunity to introduce herself as the new principal of Lincoln Middle School and to express her desire to take a proactive approach to building better partnerships. Later, as Roland builds a rapport with the school's new partners, he begins to take over more of the communication activities.

Amelia's letter to American Bank offers a model for a Reconnect letter.

SAMPLE RECONNECT LETTER

Mr. Stephen Morrison
Vice-president, Community Relations
American Bank
P.O. Box 4525
Houston, Texas 77019

Dear Mr. Morrison,

Good relationships like gardens should be nurtured. As the new principal of Lincoln Middle School, I want to engage local organizations and businesses in mutually beneficial activities that make our community an attractive place to live and work. The key words here are *mutually beneficial*.

One of my priorities as the new principal is to be proactive in our community relations. I have appointed Mr. Roland Carter, the school's assistance principal, to serve as the coordinator of our new Lincoln Middle School PAL (Partners Allied for Learning) program. Lincoln Middle School PAL members include local businesses and civic organizations that work together to make our school an asset to the community. PAL activities are also good network opportunities among our community organizations.

I have enclosed an invitation to our next PAL breakfast meeting on Tuesday, November 7, at 8:30 a.m. in the school assembly room. Ms. Mira Taylor of Reliance Realty, a Lincoln Middle School PAL, will be speaking about the new residential project under development in our community.

Good schools benefit the entire community. I believe that by working together we can complement each other's objectives. Please join us. It will give you an opportunity to meet some of our PAL members. If you have time, Roland or I can give you a tour of our school.

Sincerely,
Amelia Flores
Principal

Amelia's letter begins with an interesting sentence designed to catch Mr. Morrison's attention and prompt him to keep reading. Avoid staid, over-used phrases such as "The purpose of this letter . . ." or "I would like to take this opportunity . . ." Your opening sentences does not have to be one that will be quoted for decades, it just needs to be interesting enough to motivate the reader to continue reading. In the remaining sentences of the paragraph Amelia sets out the purpose of her letter in a way that recognizes the common interests of the school, businesses, and the community. Amelia emphasizes that partnerships must be mutually beneficial.

In the second paragraph, Amelia confirms her intention to take an active role in working with the community by describing the specific action she has taken already. She introduces Roland Carter so Mr. Morrison will be aware of his role in building partnerships.

In addition to the details of the event, the third paragraph informs Mr. Morrison that if he attends the breakfast, he may learn some useful business information about the new housing project. As a businessperson, Mr. Morrison can recognize an opportunity for networking in this gathering.

In the final paragraph, Amelia calls attention to the benefits of working together to provide good schools to the community. She suggests a tour to indicate pride in the school and a desire to have Mr. Morrison see firsthand the level of service the school is providing to students.

Amelia enclosed a newsletter to show Mr. Morrison who the current partners are, what their level of activity is, and how the school recognizes them.

Companies may be more willing to participate when they see that others are involved.

The Lincoln Middle School marketing team has categorized the Reach Out group as those businesses that are new to the community and those that have been in the community for some time but the school has never contacted. New businesses will receive a "welcome to the neighborhood" letter. Established businesses will receive a "get acquainted" letter.

SAMPLE WELCOME LETTER

Ms. Marianne Phillips
Phillips Public Relations
9735 Sycamore Street
Houston, Texas 77019

Dear Ms. Phillips.

Welcome to our community! Mira Taylor of Reliance Realty suggested I contact you to introduce myself. I am the new principal of Lincoln Middle School.

We at Lincoln Middle School believe that by working with the businesses and organizations as partners in our community we not only improve the learning environment for our children but also provide our partners with an opportunity for positive interaction with our parents, staff members, and each other. Our goal is to make our community a place where people want to live and work.

I invite you to visit our school and to attend our monthly PAL (Partners Allied for Learning) breakfast. I have enclosed an invitation to our next PAL breakfast on November 7th. Mira will be speaking about the new residential project under development in our community. Also included are our school brochure and one of our newsletters.

I hope to have the opportunity to meet you soon. Please feel free to call me or Mr. Roland Carter, Assistant Principal, who serves as the coordinator of the Lincoln PAL program.

Sincerely,
Amelia Flores
Principal, Lincoln Middle School

Enclosure

P.S. In addition to the invitation, I have enclosed a copy of the latest Lincoln Middle School newsletter. On the cover page is a story about the beginning of school Open House in which several of our PAL members participated.

In the "welcome" letter to Marianne Phillips, Amelia begins with an enthusiastic welcome and then immediately gives the name of a school partner,

Mira Taylor, as a reference. This is important because as a new business, Ms. Phillips is probably receiving many "welcome" letters. Amelia wants to alert her that this letter is different. Without a reference, Amelia might begin her letter with a statement about the advantage of getting to know the community through involvement with the school. For example, "As a new business, we know you want to get acquainted with the people in the community as quickly as possible. At Lincoln Middle School we try to bring community businesses together through our Lincoln Middle School PAL program."

In the following paragraphs, Amelia states the benefits of becoming involved with the school, invites Ms Phillips to a partner breakfast, introduces Roland Carter, and provides information about the school. Amelia includes the school newsletter and other material that contain additional information about school partnerships so Ms. Phillips can see how the school supports it partners.

The "Get Acquainted" letter below follows the same format except here Amelia acknowledges the owner's busy schedule and offers an invitation to a school open house where he can meet parents and other businesses partners.

The purpose of these letters is to express the school's desire to work with local organizations for the benefit of all. Some will be interested, some will not. It may require several invitations before a person chooses to or is able to attend. Keep in contact with these groups by continuing to send invitations to events and including them in your regular newsletter mail-out.

SAMPLE GET-ACQUAINTED LETTER

Mr. Tom Hogan
Complete Auto Service Center
5656 Washington Avenue
Houston, Texas 77019

Dear Mr. Hogan,

Introductions are always better in person, but I know you have a busy schedule so permit me to introduce myself via this letter. I am the new principal of Lincoln Middle School. I served as Assistant Principal of Lincoln Middle School for three years prior to assuming my new duties.

As the new principal of Lincoln Middle School, I believe one of our school goals should be to engage local organizations and businesses in mutually beneficial activities that make our community an attractive place to live and work. The key words here are *mutually beneficial.*

As a first step, I would like to invite you to visit our school during our Winter Holiday Open House on Tuesday, December 3, from 5:30 to 7:30 P.M. In addition to acquainting you with our school, the event will give you an opportunity to meet parents and our school's business partners. I have enclosed an invitation and one of our school brochures.

I hope we will see you at our Open House.

Sincerely,
Amelia Flores
Principal, Lincoln Middle School

Enclosure

Mr. Morrison and Ms. Phillips respond that they will be attending the next PAL breakfast. The marketing team has information packets prepared for them. The packet includes the latest copy of the school's annual report, a copy of a newspaper article about PAL sponsorship of an event, a schedule of coming events at the school, names and addresses of PAL members, and a survey (Sample Partner Survey in this chapter) for new members. Roland will use the survey information to identify perceptions about the school, improve the partnership program, and identify those groups that are willing to contribute and the level of contribution.

On the day of the breakfast, the school has designated parking for the PAL Breakfast participants with signage indicating the spaces. A sign on an easel at the entrance to the school announces the PAL breakfast and directs attendees to the school assembly room. Roland and Amelia greet the members. Each attendee has a preprinted name badge with the PAL logo.

Roland introduces the new guests to the other members and ensures that they are included in the breakfast conversation. At the beginning of the meeting, Amelia asks the new visitors, Mr. Morrison and Ms. Phillips, to take a minute to tell the group something about themselves and their companies. At the conclusion of the meeting, Roland and Amelia ask if their new visitors would like to see the school. Mr. Morrison declines, but Ms. Phillips has a child entering middle school next year and she accepts. Amelia takes her on a tour while Roland escorts Mr. Morrison to the school entrance and encourages him to attend the next PAL breakfast.

Meetings such as the PAL breakfast provide advantages to the school and the businesses. As participants attend the meetings, they see the school firsthand. A clean, orderly facility and a friendly, helpful staff will create a positive impression. The meetings are an opportunity to highlight special school and student projects and accomplishments.

It is important that the topics discussed in the meetings relate to the community, not just the needs of the school. The meetings should provide a forum for exchange of information and a place to network.

Attendees have an opportunity to interact and build relationships among themselves. A member may be interested in talking with Mr. Morrison about a new program the bank has for small businesses. Ms. Phillips may find potential clients for her new public relations firm. Finally, attendees see the school as a supportive and active community participant.

Below is a sample of a survey that can help you gather information about local businesses and their interest in partnering with the school.

LINCOLN MIDDLE SCHOOL

COMMUNITY PARTNERSHIP SURVEY

Lincoln Middle School is always interested to learn how we can improve our relationships with our business community. By completing this survey, you can let us know how our school can be a better partner to the businesses and organizations of our community. The enclosed questionnaire was designed to gather information that we can use to achieve the level of service our community partners expect and deserve. The survey will take you approximately 10–15 minutes. Thank you for your participation in this very important effort.

Please provide any additional comments, suggestions, or information that can help us improve how we serve our community. We appreciate your time and comments. Thank you!

One of Amelia's priorities is to improve the physical appearance of Lincoln Middle School. Over the years, the school's appearance has deteriorated and some residents in the surrounding area have complained. Amelia also knows that prospective parents and students may judge the quality of education inside by the way the school looks outside.

At the monthly meeting of the marketing team, Amelia tells them that she wants to initiate a project to improve the "curb appeal" of Lincoln Middle School. Working with Roland, the team defines the goals and works out a plan to implement the project through community support.

The marketing team decides to call the project "Grow With Us." The team establishes a timeline of three months from initiation to completion. A marketing team member contacts the host of a radio garden show for advice on landscaping. The radio host puts the member in contact with a teacher at a local community college who agrees to assign the school's landscaping needs as a class project. Students agree to work out a landscaping plan that will achieve the school's goals; determine the labor, materials, and funds needed; and supervise the installation.

Next, the marketing team determines how external and internal groups can participate. Working with the college students' estimate of labor, materials, and funds, the marketing team generates a list of potential partners.

Name:

Title:

Company/Organization

Address:

City/State/Zip:

Please circle your answers

How often have you visited our school?

Never   1 or 2 times   Several times   Often

If you have visited our school, please answer the following questions. What was the overall impression of the school?

Very good   Good   Fair   Poor

What was the impression of the service provided by the school staff?

Very helpful   Somewhat helpful   Not very helpful

Have you ever contacted the school by telephone or through our Website?

Never   1 or 2 times   Several times   Frequently

How would you rate the level of response provided by school staff members?

Very good   Good   Fair   Poor

Has your company or organization made any contributions to the school?

Yes   No

If yes, what were the contributions?

Services Goods   Funds

How would you rate the school's involvement with your contributions?

Very good   Good   Fair   Poor

Would your company or organization be agreeable to future participation with our school?

Yes   No

Have you attended any functions that the school holds for it business partners?

Yes   No

If yes, how would you rank the effectiveness of these functions?

Very good   Good   Fair   Poor

Please circle any of the following ways your company would like to participate.

Display student work   Donate equipment   Donate supplies

Mentoring   Scholarships   Company tours

Internships   Sponsor field trips   Be a guest speaker

Display school posters   Student incentive programs

Provide seminars related to your business for students, parents, teachers

Purchase school supplies for needy children

Other

(Use this list to address specific needs of the school, students, and parents. Do not list items or activities that the school is not prepared to utilize)

Please circle all of the following ways that Lincoln Middle School may reciprocate your contributions

Recognition on school marquee   Recognition on school website

Recognition in the school newsletter

Complimentary tickets to school events

Recognition in annual report

Recognition in community papers

Use of school facilities

Lincoln MS PAL poster for your business

Other

Figure 3.1   Community Partnership Survey

The team writes the following proposal and letter:

SAMPLE PROJECT PROPOSAL

Lincoln Middle School

Grow With Us Project

Purpose

The purpose of the *Grow With Us* project is to improve the appearance of Lincoln Middle School for the benefit of our students and the community through new landscaping.

Goals

To improve the existing landscaping through plant pruning and removal and soil renovation
To enhance the existing landscaping with new plants
To provide screening of unattractive storage areas on school grounds with shrubs
To improve the lawn and play area with low-maintenance ground cover and stepping stones

Activity

On a selected Saturday in April, Lincoln Middle School will host a Planting Day to landscape our school grounds. School staff member, students, parents, and volunteers, with the supervision of plant and landscape experts, will remove dead and diseased plants, prune existing plants, and plant new ones. The PTO will provide drinks and box lunches. Volunteers will receive t-shirts with sponsors' names. Lincoln Middle School will provide recognition in several mediums including coverage in local publications.

Benefits

- Provide surrounding residents and businesses with a visually pleasing view
- Create an inviting environment for students, staff, and visitors
- Allow children to learn about horticulture and experience the joy of seeing their work literally grow
- Build an increased pride in our school
- Create a sense of ownership and responsibility among staff and students for maintenance of our school grounds

- Establish a visible expression of what community members working together can do
- Provide an opportunity for positive recognition of our Lincoln PAL (Partners Allied for Learning) Program

LINCOLN MIDDLE SCHOOL CONTRIBUTIONS

Coordination of the project
Volunteer labor (students, staff members, parents, and school volunteers)
Water, soft drinks, sandwiches, and other snacks on Planting Day
Design of the event t-shirt
Recognition of project sponsors in a variety of mediums:
    Local media coverage
    Article in school newsletter
    Recognition on marquee
    Signage in front of school

CONTRIBUTIONS NEEDED

Plants (flowers and shrubs) and grass
Planting soil/sand
Mulch
Stepping stones
Event t-shirts with sponsors' name for volunteers
Plant experts to speak to children prior to Planting Day
Volunteers for Planting Day
Gardening equipment loan

CURRENT PARTICIPATING PARTNERS

Students from the Mr. Simon Randolph's landscape design class at Coastal Community College volunteered to create a landscape design. Students will serve as supervisors on Planting Day.

Northside Voice will publicize the Grow With Us project and Planting Day before and after the event.

The Northside Garden Club volunteered to provide students with information about planting and plant care. Members are contributing plants from their own gardens.

The Northside Homeowners Association has several members who have volunteered to bring their own tools and help on Planting Day.

All of us at Lincoln Elementary sincerely thank you for your consideration of this proposal, and we greatly appreciate any contribution you can make. We are proud to have you as a PAL and we want you to be proud of us. Thank you.

The proposal for "Grow With Us" clearly articulates the purpose and goals and defines the contributions of Lincoln Middle School and those needed from partners. The proposal also informs potential partners that work on the project is under way and that some partners are already on board.

One PAL that the school will contact is SeismaTech. Information on the partner profile indicates that the president of SeismaTech is very interested in projects that get children involved in outdoor activities. Amelia sends a personalized letter (see below a sample proposal letter) and a proposal to Kathryn Simpson, the designated contact at SeismaTech.

SAMPLE PROPOSAL LETTER

Ms. Kathryn Simpson
Director of Public Relations
SeismaTech, Corp.
P.O. Box 12345
Houston, Texas 77019-2345

Dear Ms. Simpson,

It is said that, "Beauty is only skin deep," but in our case we need to get to the roots of the problem. Our outward beauty is in need of repair and people are beginning to notice. In an effort to be a good neighbor and to increase community pride in our school, Lincoln Middle School has launched our *Grow With Us* project to beautify our school grounds with new landscaping this spring.

Through the *Grow With Us* project, we will construct a more pleasant learning environment for our students and provide them with the opportunity to experience the joy of creating a garden. Moreover, our neighbors will have a more pleasant view of us.

SeismaTech has been so generous in its efforts to introduce nature to our children we thought you would be interested in our *Grow With Us* project. We are currently developing our promotion materials and would like to include SeismaTech as one of our sponsors. I would appreciate the opportunity to discuss *Grow With Us* with you.

Enclosed is a proposal for *Grow With Us*. Roland Carter or I will call you next week to discuss your level of involvement.

Sincerely,
Amelia Flores

Principal, Lincoln Middle School

Enclosure

Amelia begins her letter to SeismaTech with a sentence that will catch the reader's attention. In the first paragraph, she establishes the need and the school's desire to be a good member of the community by addressing the need. The second paragraph describes the benefits to the students and the community. In the last paragraph, Amelia personalizes the letter to recognize SeismaTech's past involvement and their interest in children and the outdoors. Mention of the promotion materials urges SeismaTech to indicate their intention to participate in order to receive pre-event publicity. In the last sentence, Amelia sets up the next step to include SeismaTech in the project. If Ms. Simpson knows that within five to seven days Amelia will contact her, she is more likely to address the issue promptly.

With modifications, you can use this letter for all groups and individuals the team contacts. A generic variation may be created as a cover for proposals to be distributed at presentations.

After the initial letters are sent, Roland begins calling to confirm participation. He also makes presentations to a civic group and a local church that have expressed an interest. A date is set for Planting Day. With a specific date, Roland can set up a timeline for activities and delegate responsibilities to marketing team members.

Activities include completion of promotional materials with sponsors names, delivery and storage of donated materials, ordering of event t-shirts, press releases for pre-event coverage, and coordination of PTO participation. Teachers plan classroom activities to generate student enthusiasm. An alternative day is selected in the event of severe weather. Updated information regarding the event is on the school website and Facebook page, and tweets are sent to announce new participants, donations, and progress.

In the days before the event, Roland reconfirms with all groups involved including the local media. On Planting Day, everything is in place waiting for volunteers to begin work.

During the Planting Day, Roland and the marketing team constantly monitor the activities to ensure that volunteers have the supplies they need. Students receive special plants and their own planting bed. A marketing team member takes photographs throughout the day. A local television crew shows up during the afternoon to the surprise and delight of the volunteers. At the end of the day, Amelia and Roland gather the volunteers and supporters to express their thanks and unfurl an appreciation banner with the names of all supporters to place in front of the school.

After the event, Amelia and Roland send thank-you letters (sample thank-you letter is given below) to all individuals and groups that participated in the project. Roland secures post-event media coverage with photographs and sends copies of articles to all supporters. The school's subsequent newsletter, Facebook page, and website provide extensive coverage of the event. A message of appreciation is on the school marquee. The school will include a summary of the project with photographs in the next annual report.

Roland and the marketing team meet to evaluate the event. They outline factors that contributed to its success and discuss improvements for future events.

SAMPLE THANK-YOU LETTER

[NAME]
[TITLE]
[COMPANY]
[ADDRESS]
[CITY, STATE, ZIP]

DEAR [NAME]

Everything is coming up roses and petunias and daisies and lot of other plants and shrubs that make up our beautiful new school landscaping. Without your help, it would not have been a success. Thank you!

The children are so proud of their new school grounds. I heard one student proudly point out the plants, by name, that he had planted. It is amazing how much our new environment has lifted everyone's school spirit.

In case you did not see the pre-event publicity in the paper, I have enclosed a copy of the article for you. Keep an eye out for the post-event article, with pictures, that should appear within the next few days. In addition, we are announcing the names of our sponsors on our school marquee and posting news about the event via social media.

On behalf of Lincoln Middle School students, parents, and employees, I want to say how much we appreciate your support.

Sincerely,
Amelia Flores
Principal, Lincoln Middle School

Enclosure

Because of their careful preparation, attention to detail and professional approach, the Lincoln Middle School marketing team had a successful project that will benefit the school, the neighborhood, and their partners. Groups and individuals will be more receptive to helping the school in the future.

When looking for external partners, school administrators must consider how much they are willing to contribute toward building relationships. Like any successful relationship, there needs to be an understanding of the nature of the relationship, the obligations attached to it, and a commitment to making it work. As one corporate sponsor told me, "We are not an impersonal organization that simply dispenses funds upon request. We are people who, for whatever reason, have decided to make some level of commitment to public education. Our expectation is that we be recognized and treated as individuals who are working towards the same goal—an improved educational environment."

Chapter 4

Public Relations, Inside and Out

The role of public relations is to support and enhance the school's marketing activities. Building goodwill, shaping the way the school is viewed, and creating public awareness of the school's accomplishments are key public relations objectives. However, as with marketing, there are misconceptions about public relations. In the early part of the twentieth century, public relations was often viewed as the "art of manipulation" associated with political propaganda, deceptive publicity stunts, speculative land deals, and distorted press releases associated with P.T. Barnum. Even today, we still hear the phrase "That's just PR" to refer to a deceptive or manipulative activity. In truth, public relations has come a long way from earlier bad acts. Public relations professionals have worked hard to gain the public's respect by raising the standards of their profession.

Public relations can add significant value to the school's marketing efforts. In its most literal interpretation, public relations involves enhancing the organization's relationships with external and internal groups or "publics." For public school districts, those groups include virtually everyone. Private, charter, and other types of schools may have a more limited universe. Relationships are enhanced through strategies and activities that seek to improve interaction, understanding, and awareness between the school and its audiences. Public relations also involves creating and maintaining a positive image. Physical appearance, employee attitudes, accessibility, and a host of other "intangibles" create an image of association for both internal and external audiences. This chapter provides ways that districts and schools can seek to change not only what they do but also how they think about the relationships that are so important to achieving their goals.

GOT CURB APPEAL?

Remember a time when you went house hunting and the appearance of the prospective house was so unappealing that you did not bother to look inside? You judged the inside without even seeing it. Have you ever picked a new restaurant because it looked elegant, romantic, or fun? Entire industries are built upon the recognition that we often judge by appearances. Judging by appearances alone may seldom be fair or correct, but the truth is how something or someone looks influences our perception of it. Businesses are very aware of the impression created by their outward appearance and they design their exteriors to appeal to the kinds of customers they wish to attract. Banks do not look like fast-food restaurants and vice versa.

Dirty windows, untrimmed shrubs, graffiti, dead or dying plants, and trash and litter are some of the elements that make a school an eyesore. An unattractive appearance creates a negative perception of the school. Parents of potential students may find the school's appearance so uninviting they do not take the time to find out about the excellent educational environment provided within. Residents in the surrounding area may find the appearance of a school and its grounds an aggravation. A situation that is not good for community relations. Visitors are forming an opinion of the school before they walk through the front door. If the opinion is negative, the job of creating a positive impression becomes harder.

Because you see your school every day, it may be difficult to judge its appearance honestly. Ask two or three individuals outside your school to give you an honest assessment. Request both a general impression of the school and specific features that affect the overall appearance. You want to know what is appealing about your school so ask for positive as well as negative impressions.

Can you imagine going to a place of business and not being able to find the entrance? What kind of impression would that make? One of the problems I sometimes encounter when visiting schools is finding the entrance. I go to an area that looks like a main entrance only to find it locked with a sign that reads, "Use south entrance." Now I have to figure out where the south side is and it is high noon. Finding the entrance is just half the problem. Next, I have to find the office.

Most schools have a sign that demands, "All visitors must register at the school office." However, the location of the office is not always clear. I have wandered around for 10–15 minutes trying to find the office. One school

I visited had its office on the second floor at the back of the building! A school office that is difficult to find gives the impression that administrators are not open to visitors. If for some reason the office cannot be located near the building entrance, display a map stating, "You Are Here" that gives clear directions.

If making improvements to the school's appearance requires major work, turn it into a school or neighborhood project. For example, if your school needs major landscaping, designate a school landscaping day on a Saturday and include school staff, students, parents and neighborhood volunteers (see the case study in chapter 3 for an example).

Do not forget the inside. Are the hallways clean and attractive? Are the drinking fountains clean? Does the cafeteria provide an appetizing atmosphere? Are the bathrooms clean? Is there an area in the school office where people can sit? Is the waiting area pleasant? Just a few plants, colorful posters, and a bowl of candy can create a pleasing environment.

Are the classrooms inviting to visitors as well as teachers and students? Are desks facing so that visitors can see children's faces instead of their backs? Is there an adult size chair for visitors?

What about the employee environment? Is the employee lounge comfortable and inviting? Does it have a microwave oven and a place to eat? Is it quiet?

Ask these questions on a regular basis. School appearance says much about school pride and the attitude toward visitors, students, and employees. Keeping the school clean and attractive is everyone's job.

SUPPORTIVE ALUMNI SPEAK VOLUMES

Alumni are products of your school. Their continued support after they have gone speaks volumes about their experiences there. Alumni can be great spokespersons for your school especially when they attribute success in later life in part to the instruction they received at the school. Ask them to speak to students about their experiences, accomplishments, or special interests. Alumni who have achieved personal or professional recognition can serve as role models and mentors. We often forget that the celebrated author, brave astronaut, or talented sports figure was once a child sitting in a classroom reading a book or learning multiplication tables. Alumni can give motivation and inspiration to the children, especially those in disadvantaged situations.

Include alumni in your school's mail-outs. If alumni live in the community, invite them to attend school events. Encourage alumni who no longer live in the area to keep apprised of what is happening at the school or district through the school's website, Facebook, or Twitter. Communicate with them about major initiatives, news about other alumni, reunions, and school events that occur around holidays when they may be in the area visiting family. Solicit comments about alumni's positive experiences in the school and ask for permission to use these statements in your promotion pieces.

CELEBRATE CULTURAL DIVERSITY

We define culture as the beliefs, practices, values, rituals, and stories that provide an unwritten, even subconscious, influence over our thinking and our behavior. Sometimes we are unaware that we think in a certain way until we encounter someone who thinks in a different way.

Cultural diversity within the school's community is an asset and a challenge. When the school reaches out and includes diverse groups, students have access to a richness of tradition and history that is real and alive. The school is a natural place for people who might not otherwise meet to come to know and learn from each other.

A culturally diverse environment provides students, teachers, and parents with the opportunity to introduce different worldviews into their thinking. Diversity opens students' minds in ways that will serve them well after they leave school. Efforts to include minority or new immigrant parents in school activities give their children a greater feeling of their own sense of belonging. The advantages of diversity are evident in the efforts many private schools employ to achieve it.

Reaching out to a culturally diverse community may pose challenges for some schools that are unsure of how to approach specific groups. Uncertainty often leads to inaction. Inaction leads to greater isolation. Here are some ways to build a welcoming environment:

- Break the language barrier. If you have traveled to a foreign country with little or no knowledge of the native language, you probably experienced the frustration of not being able to communicate well. Even if you manage to inquire adequately in the native language, "Can you tell me where to find the train station?" the response may be indecipherable to you.

  Now imagine that you are a parent in a foreign country trying to understand about unfamiliar enrollment procedures, homework, immunizations, and school regulations or trying to communicate at parent–teacher conferences and school events. Feelings of frustration and confusion might lead to avoidance.

A principal reason parents with limited English avoid interaction with the school is the language barrier. If your school has a significant number of parents or students of limited English proficiency, having bilingual capabilities is essential not only for good communication but also for good community relations. The presence of bilingual personnel expresses to parents, students, and other members of the community that their ability to communicate and participate in the school is important. If your budget does not allow you to hire special personnel, inquire in the community for someone who can speak the language and may be willing to volunteer to assist parents, help with translations, and be available at school events.

Communication channels such as newsletters, the website, and bulletins should include information in the major languages of the community. Ensure that translations are of excellent quality.

Do not forget nonverbal communication. Body language, hand gestures, touching, facial expressions, personal space differences, and voice tone are some of the nonverbal communicators that convey different meanings in different cultures.

Some cultures look each other in the eye and speak with an intensity, tone of voice, and closeness that make even some Westerners uncomfortable. For other cultures, keeping the eyes lowered is a show of respect for the other person's status; to Americans, it may indicate someone is lying or being evasive. Once in the midst of a lively dinner party discussion in Japan, I forgot myself and lightly touched the coat sleeve of the Japanese man sitting next to me. He reacted as if I had stuck him with a pin. My action and his reaction changed the mood of the discussion to one less engaging.

- Colors may convey different cultural meanings. While black is the color of mourning in Western culture, in Japan and many Asian countries white symbolizes mourning. Certain symbols and gestures can have unintended consequences. It would be advantageous to learn something about the meaning of nonverbal communication for groups that have a significant presence in your community. In these days of global trade, considerable information about cultural dos and don'ts is easily available.
- Become culturally proactive. Provide welcome posters, main telephone messages, and website information in the major languages represented in your school or district. Encourage students to share information about special holidays and holiday customs, special foods, and music. Acknowledge holidays, such as the Chinese New Year or Cinco de Mayo, with artwork, displays, and entertainment. Develop relationships with

specialty media (newspapers, radio, and television stations) that focus on specific groups within the community. Invite them to school events and keep them informed on what is happening in the school.

Holding gatherings exclusively for new immigrant groups can increase participation. One district with over two hundred Vietnamese families held a special back-to school event on a Saturday afternoon to help parents get their children ready for school. Large welcome signs in Vietnamese greeted the parents and Vietnamese music played in the background. Vietnamese speakers conducted the program. In addition to school information, the parents received information on community programs and organizations. Coverage of the event by both English and Vietnamese media communicated to the Vietnamese community at large the school's desire to welcome parents. The benefit of the event was evident in the increased participation in the school of parents and the Vietnamese community.

Being culturally proactive also means consideration of the needs and desires of students. In Texas, where I live, support for high school football often matches religious fervor. Therefore, it was heretical when a high school principal completely abandoned football in favor of soccer. Gone were the football team and the marching band. The reason for this bold action was the high school's diverse student population that comprises 70 countries and 42 languages. Most of the students are from countries in Africa, Latin America, and Asia where soccer, not football, is the number one sport. A mariachi band now performs while the students play soccer and not one student or parent has complained.

• Seek help from cultural or religious leaders. Imagine being displaced from the homeland you have always known and placed in a new cultural situation where you are uncomfortable with the language, unfamiliar with the customs, and unsure of how to get even the most basic things done. The natural thing to do is take refuge within a group or community with people like yourself.

Families that have lived in a community for years may still feel alienated from the community outside their own. Such isolation is detrimental both to the students and to their parents. Knowing how to get through to them is not always easy. Leaders within cultural and religious communities can provide valuable information, support, and credibility for school outreach efforts.

Source credibility is important to persuasive communication. Community and religious leaders can be a voice that lends credibility to school communication. Bilingual community members can serve as the conduit for free-flowing, two-way communication and help the school with language barriers that inhibit communication.

Invite leaders to participate in your key communicators group, include them in your mailing list for newsletters and invitations to school events, notify them of the achievement of students from their ethnic or religious community. Ask them to publicize school events in their own newsletters and bulletins. Seek their advice when reaching out to parents and businesses.

• Celebrate diversity in many ways. Look for as many ways as you can to celebrate the diversity of the school internally and externally:

o Incorporate holidays such as Cinco de Mayo and Chinese New Year into class assignments and school activities.

o If the town or community has a parade, participate with a float that exemplifies the school's diversity.

o Create an exhibition of student artwork, family photographs, traditional costumes, and cultural artifacts that represent the various cultural groups in the school and display it in a local bank or library.

o Include ethnic foods, music, and artwork at school events.

o Take field trips to cultural museums and special cultural or art exhibits in your area.

o Ask people in the area with special knowledge or experiences in cultural history, art, music, anthropology, or dance to speak to students.

o Ensure that all school publications and other communication channels such as the website and videos promote the diversity of the student population through photographs, artwork, cultural event announcements, and language.

WELCOME ALL

The school can get information about new families moving into the community through its relationships with realtors and apartment complexes, or it can get the information from local government agencies. Send preprinted welcome cards to newcomers. Include the school website address, names of key administrators, and contact information. Put newcomers' names and addresses in your database.

A beginning of school event is a good way to make newcomers to the neighborhood feel welcome and acquaint them with your school. Do not restrict the invitations just to people with children in your school. Include all newcomers, individuals, and businesses. They are potential volunteers and school supporters.

Have someone at the door to greet people and make them feel welcome. Have brochures available to hand out. Also, provide information that newcomers will find helpful such as maps, and information on local services, businesses, and civic organizations (a good way to promote school partners). Have a sign-in sheet so that you can get names and addresses of those who come.

Inviting newcomers also gives the school's external partners such as civic groups and businesses the opportunity to introduce themselves to new neighbors in a positive way.

REACH OUT TO NEW PARENTS

Pre-K, kindergarten, and elementary schools can make use of available birth records to reach out to new parents. Send a congratulatory note or letter that includes information about the school and an invitation to visit. Add the new parents to your mailing list for regular communication. Invite them to any open house or events the school is having.

Once a year invite mothers of babies and toddlers to a panel discussion or workshop on ways they can prepare them for school by developing their cognitive abilities through activities at home. Include on the panel teachers, counselors, and district specialists who can discuss new ideas, offer suggestions, and answer questions. Have information on related books, websites, toys, and activities available.

VISITOR PARKING SAYS "WELCOME"

Have you ever stopped patronizing a business or restaurant because parking was just too much of a hassle? That is why restaurants and even some businesses provide valet parking.

When conducting marketing workshops, frequently, I am required to circle the school several times before finding a spot a couple of blocks away to park, then lug my presentation booklets, laptop, and other materials down cracked sidewalks, over curbs, through parking lots to reach the school.

Many of the parents who visit your school, especially elementary schools, have toddlers or babies in strollers with them. Having to park a block or two away is an irritation and a hardship. Older volunteers may find walking even a couple of blocks in extreme heat or cold taxing and even harmful.

To those of you who have parking spaces designated for visitors, my congratulations! To those of you who do not, consider the impression it makes on visitors. If you truly want to make visitors feel welcome at your school, provide spaces for them to park and have the parking spaces clearly marked.

WHEN A NOTE FROM THE PRINCIPAL'S OFFICE IS A GOOD THING

Too often communication with parents falls solely on teachers. A personal note from the principal to parents and students acknowledging outstanding achievement speaks volumes about the school's appreciation of excellence. Writing a brief note takes only a few minutes, but its effect on the parents and student is lasting. A note of appreciation to a volunteer or employee goes a long way toward keeping him motivated. Not only does a note from the principal add special recognition for accomplishment, it also creates a positive communication channel.

To minimize the time required to "think of what to say," create several standard notes then adapt them to the specific situation. If your handwriting is difficult to read, type them, but always sign them personally.

DONUTS, COFFEE, AND A "GOOD MORNING"

A good way for administrators and staff members to meet parents at the beginning of the school year is to offer donuts and coffee or bottled juice to parents as they drop off their children for school. Even if the principal has time only to introduce himself or herself and say a few words, it shows that the school welcomes them.

It is especially important to have positive interaction with those parents who, for whatever reason, are not active in the school—the working parent who does not have time, the newcomer who feels like an outsider, or the foreign-born parent who feels uncomfortable. A friendly "Good morning," a smile, and a cup of coffee from school staff members is one more way to connect with parents. By timing this activity with an upcoming event, such as Parent Night, staff members can use the interaction to publicize the event and encourage parents to attend.

VIDEOS FOR FUN AND PROMOTION

Videos are a powerful communication medium. Images accompanied by sound attract and hold people's attention. The ability to duplicate and distribute videos simply and cheaply on DVDs or put them on your website makes them especially appealing.

Large school districts may have departments that provide this service for schools; but new high-quality, easy-to-use video equipment and software make creating videos possible for smaller districts and schools. If your budget does not allow for the purchase of new equipment, look for used equipment in the classified ads or run an ad asking for equipment. Check with local colleges, companies, or television stations that may be replacing equipment and are willing to donate their old. Camera stores generally have used equipment from trade-ins at significant discounts.

Videos should have a professional look. A video that looks like someone's bad home movie is counterproductive. If the school or district does not have someone who can produce quality videos, solicit help from local businesses who have expertise in videography, advertising, and public relations. Companies may not be willing to donate all their work, but they may offer a heavily discounted rate if the school recognizes their contribution prominently on the video and in other school communications. Remind them that not only will parents see the video but also local organizations, other businesses, and the community at large. Allow them to use the video as an example of their work in their own marketing materials.

Check with radio/television departments of local colleges and universities. Professors and students may be willing to work with the school as a class or department project. Do not hesitate to ask for samples of their work. If it is good, they will want you to see it.

Use videos to promote the district or school to parents of potential students, help local civic associations promote the benefits of the community to attract new businesses, solicit support from local organizations, generate school spirit at events, and recruit quality employees. Videos can also recognize academic achievements, articulate the district's vision, recognize community support, provide new student orientation, and acknowledge the dedication of employees. Use the same communication guidelines that you apply to your other promotion material: Keep it short (about two to three minutes), keep it relative, keep it viewer focused, and keep it moving. Use real students, parents, and employees, not actors.

Use videos in presentations, include them in information packets to prospective students and their parents, add them to annual reports, make them a part of school tours, and show them at school rallies.

One middle school I worked with made weekly videos in a "morning news" format of students making announcements, recognizing special achievements, and reporting on activities with its community partners. The video was then played on a continuous loop on a television set up in the school's office for visitors.

VIDEOS FOR ABSENT PARENTS

Missing a recital, special sporting event, or play is always a disappointment to parents and children. The next best thing to having a parent there is being able to enjoy the moment together at home with a video of the event. Parents and students will appreciate the effort the school has made to allow them to share these special times.

Make a video of special school events, then loan the videos for a specified time or ask parents to provide a blank tape to the school for a duplicate that they can keep. Do not loan the original. Keep originals in a permanent file to provide a visual history of school events. Excerpts from the videos may be used in other promotional videos.

COLLABORATING TO MAXIMIZE YOUR MARKETING EFFORT

Collaboration is an organized effort that benefits all participants both individually and as a whole. Through collaboration, schools can maximize their resources, enhance their marketing efforts, and yet remain competitive.

Magnet schools can jointly promote the excellence of magnet programs and the advantages that specialized classes provide to students after graduation, whether in the workplace or in a university. Generally, these schools do not compete for the same students. A magnet school for the fine arts is not likely to lure away a student who is interested in engineering. Collaborating on promotional materials such as brochures, videos, and presentations can maximize their resources.

Elementary, middle, and high schools in the same feeder patterns can market their schools as a continuum of excellence through shared programs and activities. A common logo, slogan, colors, and mission allows for consistency in the look and content of promotional materials.

All schools with common religious beliefs—for example, Episcopal schools of San Antonio or Islamic schools of Houston—may market their ability to give students an elementary through high school education in their faith. Marketing materials could be distributed through local churches or mosques.

All the schools in a district can work together to promote the excellence of their schools and the district's benefits to the community. The district may conduct a branding initiative through a collective marketing effort that includes and benefits all schools.

A BOOKMARK CAN DO MORE THAN MARK A BOOK

Use bookmarks to promote reading, the school, and school supporters (figure 4.1). Hand out the bookmarks at the beginning of school when textbooks are issued. Give a supply of bookmarks to local bookstores and other businesses to hand out to customers. Pass them out at PTO meetings or at presentations to local groups. Distribute bookmarks to parents at the beginning of school.

This promotion vehicle can be virtually cost free when you collaborate with local businesses to underwrite it. Use one side to promote learning and reading and the other side to acknowledge your sponsor or sponsors. Below is suggested text for bookmarks.

10 Ways to Help Your Child Learn

Provide a quiet study area for your child.
Set aside a certain time each day for study.
Look at your child's work and give positive feedback.
Provide reference books and other supplies.
Show an interest in what your child is learning.
Take your child to the library, museum, zoo, etc.
Play games with your child.
Meet your child's teacher.
Limit television time and computer games.
Celebrate your child's accomplishments.

10 Reasons to Read to Your Child

Your child will connect reading to a positive experience.
You create a physical closeness.
It increases your child's vocabulary.
You introduce new subjects in an enjoyable way.
It is a good way to teach values.
It builds your child's imagination.
It is a time your child has you to himself/herself.
It helps your child learn to read.
The illustrations encourage creativity.
You might learn something.

**10 Reasons
to
Read to Your Child**

1. Your child connects reading to a positive experience

2. You create a physical closeness with your child

3. It increases your child's vocabulary

4. You introduce new subjects in an enjoyable way

5. It's a good way to teach values

6. It builds your child's imagination

7. It's a time your child has to him/herself

8. It helps your child learn to read

9. The illustrations promote creativity

10. You might learn something too

Lincoln Middle School

3456 Elm Street
Houston, TX 77007
Lincolnms.edu

Lincoln Middle School PAL
(Partners Allied for Learning)

Encourage parents to

READ TO YOUR CHILD

Bookworm Books

Young Readers' Book Nook

Emily's Used Books

Green's Stationery

Best Office Supply

Lincoln MS PTO

Riverview Public Library

Food Basket Supermarket

Reliant Realty

Lincoln Middle School

3456 Elm Street
Houston, TX 77007
Lincolnms.edu

Figure 4.1   Example of Promotion Bookmark

SPEND SOME TIME AT THE MALL

Set up a table at a local mall on a Saturday afternoon for two to three hours or at a local grocery store after work hours, 5:30 p.m. to 7 p.m., to distribute information about your school, meet parents, sign up volunteers, and find potential business partners. This activity is an effective way to get out of the office and promote your school on a personal level.

Set up a table and staff the table with an administrative person (principal, assistant principal, or business manager) and a teacher or volunteer. Older students may also participate. Put a school banner on the front of the table and set a poster on an easel to identify your school. Have materials such as brochures, newsletters, information about volunteer programs and volunteer forms, announcements about upcoming events, information about community partnership programs, and PTO materials available. Bring business cards. Use an inexpensive giveaway (pencils, bookmarks, bumper stickers) as a way to make initial contact. Do not get involved in lengthy discussions or complaints about specific students, programs, or issues. Instead, invite the individual to set up a meeting with the appropriate person at the school. Keep your presence upbeat and positive.

REMEMBER THAT *EVERYONE IS IN MARKETING*

Rude or indifferent employees can undermine the best-planned and -executed marketing strategies. It is important that employees understand that everyone plays a role in making the school's marketing effort a success.

There are a number of ways to make employees aware of their part in the marketing and public relations effort:

- Keep them informed via memos or reports at regular meetings about marketing activities, special visitors coming to the school, new school partners, or upcoming promotions.
- Solicit their ideas and suggestions.
- Make them ambassadors of the school within their own communities. What they say to family, friends, and neighbors has an impact on how the school is perceived. People will often look to them, rather than school administrators, for the "real story."
- Get them involved in some of the "fun" activities involved in marketing, not just the mundane tasks.
- Ensure that they receive credit when a marketing project or initiative is successful.

IF THE SCHOOL CULTURE IS TOXIC, DETOX

We define culture by the beliefs, values, practices, rituals, and stories that reflect and influence the way we think and behave. Organizations, like individuals, have cultures and the people in them conduct themselves within a framework of behavior that reflects the organization's cultural beliefs.

As an organization, a school has a culture. If the culture is positive, the environment is conducive to learning, teaching, and serving the needs of the students, the employees, the parents, and the community. Although there is no one best culture, some of the characteristics that would reflect a positive school culture would be a willingness to improve and grow individually and collectively through change, a commitment to service, a collaborative approach to problem solving and decision-making, a respect for and a recognition of achievement, and courtesy toward and respect for others.

A negative culture not only impedes progress internally, it also affects the school's relationship with the community. One of the most common is a "them versus us" mentality, which may pit office staff against teachers, teachers against parents, administrators against the community, and teachers against each other. The result is an organization working against itself to the detriment of all.

Because an organization's culture is so essential to its success or failure, it is important that schools assess their culture and make changes accordingly. Ask each member of the school's marketing team to write down five adjectives or short phrases that describe the school. The descriptions may be positive or negative. Who are the role models at the school? What criteria define something as "good"? What are the reoccurring ceremonies and rituals at the school? What do they symbolize? How would the team describe them? Obligatory? Fun? Boring? Stressful? Ask employees and students to participate in a similar exercise. Compare the results. What cultural characteristics become evident? If the team feels it needs more assistance in defining the culture, information on culture surveys and books on the subject are available on the Internet.

Next, define the kind of culture the school wants to have and cultivate it. What aspects of the present culture contribute to the desired culture? What aspects detract from the desired culture?

If a desired cultural characteristic is *innovative*, what is the school presently doing to instill, encourage, and celebrate innovation? What aspects in the present culture hinder or discourage innovation? What can be done to change those aspects? Begin to shape the new culture through daily words and actions. Celebrate examples of innovation. Recognize innovative thinking and action through stories in the school newsletter. Put up posters with quotes related to creative or original thinking. Provide books, videos, and training that help staff members develop an innovative perspective.

It is important to remember that cultures do not develop quickly; therefore, they will not transform quickly. Some individuals will resist change. Do not try to alter too many aspects of the school's culture at once. Changing a culture, especially one that is deeply embedded, will require persistence, focus, and time.

Because cultures do not change quickly, it is often difficult to see that they are changing at all until the change becomes pervasive and evident. It is important to assess your school's culture periodically with school staff, teachers, and even the external audiences to determine if it is undergoing any significant changes. When you hear with some frequency people say, "It used to be that . . . ," listen carefully. Such statements may be indicators that there may be positive or negative cultural changes occurring.

HOW'S YOUR CUSTOMER SERVICE?

Do you know how you would be treated if you were a visitor or caller to your school? Are you sure? I have called the offices of schools and districts that prided themselves on the quality of their schools only to experience appalling customer service. Remember, few people will call back to complain, but they will complain to others or move on to where they feel more welcome.

Frontline staff members, who have the first and most frequent contact with visitors or callers, are critical to how your school is perceived. Tone of voice, body language, even personal appearance influence whether interactions are positive or negative. It is important that all school personnel understand that customer service is an essential part of marketing and that they are key people in delivering customer service. Customer service, however, extends beyond the front office. Teachers, crossing guards, counselors, and administrators need to be cognizant of the importance of good customer relations.

Make excellence in customer service a priority at your school. Periodically check the level of customer service through surveys or "testers" who call or visit the school to evaluate the level of service. It is vital to set high standards and communicate to all staff members how important they are to meeting those standards.

Do not assume that an employee knows how to provide excellent service because it seems like common sense to you. Employees may be following examples they have observed in fellow workers. Or they simply do not know what is expected of them. It is difficult for new employees to effect changes even when they know the situation in not customer friendly.

You cannot expect employees to meet expectations if they do not know what the expectations are and how to meet them. Create a handbook that clearly states correct procedure for answering the telephone, taking messages, greeting visitors, and interacting with parents, students, and fellow employees. One good way to impress upon employees the importance of customer service is with examples of good and bad customer service we all encounter in everyday life: being left on hold, being passed from one person to another, an "it's not my job" attitude, lack of interest in resolving the issue. I am sure everyone could come up with their own examples. Then ask, "How does that make you feel?" "What do you think of that business or organization after such treatment?"

You may choose to reinforce the importance of customer service by providing employees with training. Training is a non-accusatory approach to setting standards and expectations. If the school cannot afford to send employees to customer training or to have a trainer come to the school, find a video that employees can watch together or individually. There are numerous books, videos, and online training modules to help you find the right medium for your situation.

Communicate unfavorable comments about customer service in a nonconfrontational, impersonal manner. If complaints repeatedly relate to a specific individual, have a private conversation with the employee. Do not speak in generalities. Be specific about what attitudes or activities are at issue and have specific recommendations to correct them.

Do not forget to pass on praise and compliments. Employees need to hear when they are doing a great job as well as when they are not. A word or two of thanks sends a message that employees' efforts are recognized and appreciated.

24-HOUR RESPONSE TIME FOR
TELEPHONE CALLS OR E-MAILS

A response policy of 24 hours for administrators and staff members expresses that the school values communication with the community. Without a response policy, a tendency exists for communication avoidance. Ask employees to set aside a couple of times during the day to return calls and e-mails. A response, even if it is only to let the person know that the message was received, is important. A response indicates that the school is making an effort to resolve the issues, find the answers to questions and provide the requested information. If you know that someone else can respond better to a call, pass on the information with the request for a 24-hour response.

DEALING WITH DIFFICULT PEOPLE DIPLOMATICALLY

As an undergraduate student, I worked as the front desk supervisor in a hotel that was very proud of its service to guests. As a supervisor, dealing with guest complaints was my responsibility. In my three years at the hotel, I earned the equivalent of a master's degree, if not a doctorate, in dealing with difficult people. I found the following strategy to be particularly effective when dealing with unhappy or angry people:

- Do not take it personally. I know this is easy to say and difficult to do. Generally, the first reaction to an unhappy or angry person is to feel as if we are personally under attack. The person is upset because of a situation— something happened or did not happen. The situation is the issue, not you personally. It is surprising how efficient and professional you can be when you disassociate your feelings from the situation. It is difficult at first, but keep reminding yourself throughout the interaction, "This is not about me, unless I let it become about me."
- Do not make excuses. People do not want to hear excuses; they want to hear that someone cares about what has happened, appreciates their feelings, and will do what can be done to resolve the issue.
- Listen. The first thing an upset person wants is for someone to listen. Listening gives you not only information but also time to understand the situation. It also gives the upset person a chance to vent a little. Ask questions to determine if there is a single issue or if other issues are involved.

    A parent may say she is upset because her child did not make the debate team. As you listen, watch for nonverbal clues such as body language. Does the person seem angry or worried? By asking questions, you may find out that her underlying concern is that her child seems to have lost interest in school and become withdrawn. Her anger is a result of her concern.

    Sometimes a person just wants to express his feelings. He may have placed several calls to the school and received no response. His initial issue may have been minor, but now he is really upset because he perceives the school is unresponsive.

    Take notes to ensure that details are not forgotten or misinterpreted later. Clarify any points that you do not understand or that seem unusual.
- Express understanding. I have found that acknowledging a person's feelings and expressing a desire to improve the situation will quickly ease most emotional interactions. People often work themselves into an emotional state, but don't know how to work themselves out of it. You can help tone down a volatile situation by expressing an understanding for the person's feelings. Saying, "I can see how you are concerned about this," or "I understand why this would upset you," validates the person's feelings and acknowledges that an issue exists that needs to be addressed.
- Allow time for private discussion. If the person is creating an uncomfortable emotional scene in the reception area, invite him into your office. This

limits the tirade's effect on others and shows that you consider the situation important enough for your personal attention. Offer coffee, water, or a soft drink. If possible, sit in an adjacent chair rather than behind your desk. Ask office staff members not to interrupt you. Then listen.

- Aim for some initial agreement. If a person has expressed what action she wants taken, tell her what you are prepared to do and see if you can reach an agreement. If you cannot meet her requests, explain why. The goal is to achieve some kind of agreement at the time, even if it is just agreeing on what the next step should be. Be specific about what you will do. For example, "As a first step, I will speak with the debate coach, Mr. Williams, today about the selection process for the debate team and about Mary's participation. Then either Mr. Williams or I will call you. Is that acceptable?" The parent now knows what will happen and when.
- Focus on the issue. People who are angry often use the occasion to bring up other unrelated grievances. Focus on resolving the issue at hand and suggest discussing other matters later.
- Follow through. All diplomacy is negated if nothing is done to follow through on assurances. If you have assigned school staff members tasks to resolve the issue, follow up to see that they have completed them. Keep in touch with the aggrieved person until the issue is resolved.

GOODWILL BEGINS WITHIN THE SCHOOL

Public relations is not exclusively external. Successful marketing requires effective relationship management with internal groups too. Sometimes administrators spend so much time building and nurturing relationships with external audiences, they forget about one of the greatest assets or liabilities right under their noses—school employees.

Employees talk. They talk to each other, to their neighbors, their families, people in organizations to which they belong, and to people coming to or calling the school. The community may or may not believe all that they hear or read from media sources; but they likely will give credence to what they hear from someone within the school. If employees are unhappy or poorly informed, they can hinder your marketing efforts. Conversely, employees can be goodwill ambassadors who are one of the school's greatest strengths.

To ensure positive interaction with your external groups, it is important to improve the interaction among internal groups of the school. Employees and students are more likely to be friendly and helpful to external groups if a respectful, courteous, and helpful atmosphere exists internally. It is essential that school employees are treated with the same courtesy and respect that is demanded of them. It is the responsibility of the top administrators to establish the proper environment. Require and demonstrate the same principles of courtesy among internal groups as you would with external ones. Following are some suggestions that can help foster goodwill:

• Do not allow staff members to be used as scapegoats. Not only is this practice demoralizing, but it also allows people to abdicate responsibility by blaming others. When that happens, accountability is lost. If an administrator or teacher is allowed to blame the office staff members because he failed to return a parent's phone call or missed a meeting, the practice will become prevalent and responsibility meaningless. It becomes difficult for front office employees to work with parents and others if they are constantly seen as incompetent or unhelpful because they have been blamed for others' mistakes. Equally important as not blaming people for what they did not do is recognizing them for what they did do.
• Recognize employees for their work. Recognizing employees is advice that many people give and not enough follow. Educators above all should be aware of the importance of recognition. Recognition can be a simple "Thank you for your efforts," a formal certificate of appreciation, or "Employee of the Month" with a special perquisite.
• Employee of the Month should not be a popularity contest or one reserved for "special" employees. Use it to recognize real dedication or special efforts. Above all, do not allow individuals to take credit for other people's work. Often people do this under the guise of "We are all working together for the greater good," usually spouted by the person who is taking the credit. If an accomplishment was a team effort, recognize the entire team, not just the team leader. To foster creativity, innovation, and achievement, give credit where it is due.

Recognize people publicly for their work through announcements at meetings, articles in the school newsletter, an Employee Honor Role poster on an easel at the entrance to the school, or special award pin. Acknowledge the service of long-term employees and recognize their contributions in the annual report or marketing communication as an example of the quality of school personnel. Students can wear ribbons that express their appreciation for efforts of school employees: "Thank you for being here every day," "We ♥ our School Staff Members," or "You R Appreciated." Recognize employees on your school marquee. For outstanding efforts, get district-wide recognition.

Recognize custodians, cafeteria workers, and crossing guards who are sometimes overlooked in the daily routine of the school even though they play an important role in its successful operation. Students should be aware of how these employees make their school a good place to learn. Thank them with a standing ovation at a school assembly. Invite them to all school events. Provide recognition in the newsletter: "Lincoln Middle School is proud of its dedicated employees. Mr. Jones, our custodian, has been with the school for over 10 years. Last year during the January snowstorm, Mr. Jones worked long hours to keep our school secure and warm. Thank you, Mr. Jones."

The dedication of long-term employees speaks well of your school and its environment. Be visibly proud of what such dedication says about the school.

- All employees need to feel that they are a part of the school's past, present, and future success. At least once a year, hold a meeting that includes everyone, office personnel, food service workers, teachers, custodians, and volunteers. Have breakfast or lunch catered. Make it a special occasion.

Review the past year and welcome the new one, recognize outstanding work, share plans for the future, and look at the school's opportunities and obstacles. The meeting is an opportunity not only to provide information but also to listen to employees. Ask for employee input. Employees often see and hear things that those in the central office do not. Encourage them to be the eyes and ears of the school.

If you think that employees may be reluctant to speak, pass out large index cards and ask them to write their comments and questions anonymously. Provide a box, away from the front of the room, where employees can drop their cards.

The objective is to let employees know that they are essential to the organization, and, therefore, contribute to its achievements. This is a good opportunity to remind them that they too are a part of the marketing effort.

- Inform employees *first* about issues, changes, or events, which affect them directly. Whether the news is good or bad, all employees deserve to know when things are happening that affect them, and they deserve to know before others outside the organization. It is demoralizing when those outside the organization seem to know more than those inside the organization. This is especially true when the news is not good. The ill will can be devastating to your school internally and externally. Relatively minor issues can become major ones when rumors and hearsay are the main forms of communication. Give employees related details and background information so they can have an understanding of the entire situation.

When news is positive, employees can be your best "cheerleaders." Share good news in a way that makes all employees feel proud. Encourage them to share the good news with their friends, family, and neighbors.

A bulletin, "What is Happening in Our School This Week," that informs about daily happenings and a monthly employee newsletter on larger issues will keep everyone informed.

Employees can be your best supporters in difficult situations. Much good work to build positive perceptions of the school is undone when the need for employees to be informed is not considered.

- Extend small expressions of appreciation every day. Something as simple as using people's names when talking with them can make a difference in how they feel. Make a list of small gestures that express the value you put on employees' efforts and check frequently to ensure that you are matching actions with words. Below are some suggestions.
  - Remember staff members' birthdays with a card.
  - Give each employee a nameplate for her or his desk.
  - Give them copies of articles you find that are related to their jobs.
  - Provide employee training.
  - Order in pizza for everyone.
  - Give staff members plants for their desks.
  - Make popcorn one afternoon.
  - Provide personalized note pads.
  - Introduce staff members to business partners and VIPs who visit.
  - Know something about their families and ask about them.

THE "BUTTERFLY EFFECT"

In the 1960s, Edward Lorenz, an MIT meteorologist, working on chaos theory, made a stunning announcement. Lorenz proposed that the effects of a group of butterflies flapping their wings in one part of the world could spawn severe weather in a distant part of the world. The idea is that small actions can have dramatic, far-reaching effects. The idea of Lorenz's postulation has application in a number of ways. Through observation, we can see the Butterfly Effect at work every day when small things, positive and negative, trigger much larger events.

Neglecting to say "thank you" or "good job" or failing to recognize that someone put in special effort may seem like a small fault in the big scheme of running the school. However, when these oversights are sufficient in number and occur over a period of time, they can profoundly affect employee morale.

The loss of quality employees, poor customer service, negative comments outside the school, and workplace errors that result from low employee morale can have dramatic far-reaching effects that extend into the community and influence people's perceptions of the school for some time. Likewise, small gestures that create high employee morale can produce far-reaching dramatic, positive results.

If morale begins to slip or the level of efficiency drops, don't always look for the big issues, it may be something small.

THE PARENT/TEACHER MEETING

The one-on-one interaction of the parent/teacher meeting is an invaluable opportunity to positively impress your most valuable customers: parents. At the end of the meeting, parents will have formed an opinion not only of their child's teacher but of the school who employs him or her.

Parents will form a first impression with their eyes. How is the teacher dressed? What messages do her facial expressions and body language convey? Is she welcoming? Harried? Distracted? Does he seem engaged in the meeting or just going through the motions? What does the classroom look like? Is there a sense of purpose and organization? If there is equipment, is it clean, operable, and tidy?

Next comes verbal communication. Is the communication truly two way? Does the teacher speak in terms that are easy for the parents to understand? Does she use specific examples of the student's activities to clarify her points? Does he offer specific suggestions for improvement? Does the teacher give parents time to discuss their concerns, feelings, and interests related to their child? Does the teacher make comments about his perceived shortcomings of the school, other teachers, or the administration? If there needs to be follow-up, are specific actions and time frames established?

Below are some suggestions for teachers that can make the parent/teacher meeting more effective:

- Before the meeting, prepare an outline of what will be discussed and any questions you have for parents. Have examples of the student's work to show.
- Provide a folder of information such as announcements, newsletters, for the parents to take with them.
- Dress professionally.
- Make sure your classroom is orderly and clean.
- Greet the parents by standing, shaking hands, and welcoming them sincerely.

- Arrange chairs side by side around a table. Do not sit behind your desk and hand items to them.
- Be prepared for parents who may be concerned, intimidated, arrogant, or angry.
- Use simple, direct language free of jargon, sarcasm, condescension, or negativity.
- Make sure parents feel free to ask questions throughout the meeting.
- Provide concrete suggestions and recommendations.
- Summarize the meeting and agree on a schedule for any follow-up.
- If the meeting is running over schedule and you have other parents to see, set a time for further discussion.
- Thank the parents for coming.

Parents come to these meeting because they care about their children and want to know that the school does also. This is a prime opportunity for teachers to convey their personal dedication and that of the school to the needs of the students.

SCHOOL TOURS

When a friend of mine was looking for the right school for her five-year-old, she visited three schools within her area. Because the schools' academic ratings were similar, she based her decision on where to send her child solely on her tours of the schools. She explained, "How I was received, the timeliness and organization of the tour, the access to the classrooms, and the information I was given to help me make a decision told me a lot about how the school viewed me and my child."

A visit may be the first, and only, impression someone has of the school. Providing school tours is an opportunity to make the first impression a good one.

Tour guides can be administrators, staff members, volunteers, even students, but they need to be prepared to give knowledgeable, well-organized, consistent tours of the school. It is important that a person's interest in the school not be met with insufficient information, well-intentioned hype, or someone's personal issues. Give school guides the information and training to represent themselves and the school favorably.

At a minimum, a tour should include information that visitors are likely to want such as school ranking, test scores, class sizes, special programs, teacher qualifications, etc., a brief history of the school, and the school's plans. You do not want a canned speech, so give your guides key talking points and a route, and then let them add to it with their own experiences and personalities. Ask each guide to take one member of the marketing team on a practice tour.

Have prepared folders of materials visitors can take with them. Don't forget younger students who accompany their parents on the visit. Have a special packet for them with pages to color or word puzzles that are relative to the school. Include information about extracurricular activities that may of interest to older students such as sports or arts. Be sure to address student interests during the tour.

To prevent work or class interruptions, have designated days and times for tours from which visitors can choose. Above all, the visitors should leave with a feeling that your school is proud of its accomplishments and eager to welcome visitors.

It may be difficult for some parents to be away from their jobs during regular school hours. To accommodate those parents, conduct a least one tour a semester on a Saturday or after work hours. This not only allows the parents an opportunity to visit the school but also conveys that your school understands their needs and wants to accommodate them.

VOLUNTEERS IN PUBLIC SCHOOLS (VIPS)

Volunteers in schools are important not only because they give labor and expertise to the school but also because they are beneficial links with the community. Volunteers can be goodwill ambassadors outside the school environment. Too often this valuable resource is lost due to lack of appreciation and disorganization.

School volunteers have told me that they worked in a school for months before office staff members remembered their names. Other volunteers have told of showing up to work with a class only to find out that the class had gone on a field trip. No one had called the volunteers to cancel or reschedule. Who would want to continue to donate time, if no one appreciates it?

Below are some ways that the school or district can show appreciation for the contributions volunteers make.

- Have an attractive name badge on a lanyard for each volunteer.
- Take new volunteers around the school, not only to acquaint them with the school but also to acquaint the school with them.
- Occasionally, have a mid-morning or afternoon meeting with volunteers to chat with them about their experiences, solicit suggestions, or find out what is going on in the community.

- Designate a week for special recognition of volunteers' work.
- Put pictures of volunteers on display in the hallways.
- Invite them to school functions.
- Have something meaningful for them to do.
- Send them thank-you notes from the children.
- Have district-wide recognition of volunteer work with a special luncheon. Ask principals to submit candidates for a Volunteer of the Year award and announce the winner at the luncheon.
- Feature the volunteers and their work on the school website and Facebook page. Include photographs of them working with the students and teachers.
- Provide volunteer parking spaces if you can.
- Get media coverage of special projects with volunteers.
- Most of all smile and welcome volunteers when they come to the school.

VOLUNTEERING IS TWO WAY

Volunteering works two ways. When school staff members and students go out into the community as volunteers, they are creating an image of the school as a contributor and not just as a receiver of services. When school volunteers, outfitted in t-shirts with the school logo, help to clean up a local park or paint the house of an elderly person, they show that the school sees itself as a part of the community. Involving students in community service goes a long way toward dispelling any negative perceptions local residents may have of them. It is also a good opportunity to develop among the students an understanding of the importance and rewards of community service.

Contact local civic or government organizations for information on volunteer opportunities. Provide a list of volunteer opportunities to individual students and to student organizations. Give the volunteers a group name that connects to the school. Work with a school partner to provide special volunteer t-shirts. Once employees and students are involved, keep them motivated with recognition of their efforts through articles in the school newsletter and local media. Include pictures of volunteer activities on the school website, Facebook page, and in the school's annual report and brochures.

PLACE MATS AS PROMOTION

Schools report that often there are small, individually owned businesses in the community that would like to support the school, but their resources limit what they can do. Creating place mats that can be used or sold in local businesses is one way to include these willing partners in a school promotion.

Ask students to create artwork in a uniform size that would make a good place mat. On each piece of artwork, include the name of the student, his/her grade, and the teacher's name. The artwork can relate to particular school achievements or programs—for example, artwork depicting what students learned in the school's new science program or during a summer reading series or a particular event or time. Work with a local print shop to laminate the artwork to use as place mats. Be sure to recognize any contribution of materials and labor on the place mats.

Ask restaurants in the neighborhood to use the place mats for a week or a month. Announce the event and provide a list of participating restaurants in the school newsletter to acknowledge their participation and direct customers to them. Local stores can sell them or the place mats can be sold at school or community events in which the school participates as a fund-raiser.

MAKING SURE EVERYONE GETS THE PICTURE

Disposable cameras have an expiration date. Ask a local store to donate cameras reaching their expiration date to a class or grade level. Recruit a local photographer or a teacher of photography from a nearby college to make a presentation to the students on how to take good pictures. If having a guest presentation is not possible, get some photography books from the local library and make them available to the students for a week or two before the project starts.

Students then have a specified time to take pictures on a particular theme—for example, my family, my school, my neighborhood, or a class outing. To hold down costs, students can mat their own photographs.

Exhibit the photographs at multiple locations such as banks, the local library, bookstores, and the school so that each child can have at least one photograph on display. Promote the exhibition through the school newsletter, local newspaper, and communication pieces of the participating organizations. Be sure to recognize the store that donated the cameras.

MAKING YOUR APPRECIATION PUBLIC

Good relations with your local newspaper can provide the school with ways to recognize the organizations and businesses that help it. Recognition may be in the form of a letter on the op-ed page, excerpts from students' letters, or a special announcement thanking school supporters. Another option is to insert a special page in the end-of-school newsletter with a montage of students' letters thanking supporters. Send extra copies of publications to your supporters so that they may display or distribute them as well.

BE ENTERTAINING

Do not limit your student performances to singing Christmas carols in a bank lobby. Use every opportunity to get the talents of your students known in the community. Take inventory of the performance possibilities your students can offer, and then let local businesses and organizations know about them. Student bands, string quartets, jazz groups, the drama club, cultural performers, dance ensembles, or choirs can perform at business openings, civic club lunches or dinners, conferences, or community celebrations.

Unless individuals have children in school or volunteer at your school, they may have little contact with your students. When people have the opportunity to interact with or even observe the students, their involvement becomes more personal. Contact with your students may encourage people to become involved with your school or at the least have a more favorable impression.

PUTTING HOLD TIME TO GOOD USE

None of us likes to be put on hold; but, it happens. Personally, if I must be put on hold, I prefer listening to classical music, some good jazz, or even new product information rather than an annoying announcement, "Thank you for waiting. Your call is important to us. Someone will be with you shortly." It is particularly annoying when I have heard it for the fifth or sixth time. If my call is so important, why isn't someone responding to it?

Try not to make callers to your school wait too long or too often. When it is necessary, utilize the hold time to promote the businesses and organizations that support your school. For example: *Hi, my name is James. I am a student at Lincoln Middle School. All of us in the sixth grade would like to thank SeismaTech Inc., a Lincoln Middle School PAL, for sponsoring our trip*

to see the new gem and mineral collection at the Museum of Natural Science.
Seeing the real thing made our science class even more interesting. Thank
you SeismaTech, a Lincoln Middle School PAL. You can also use hold time to
promote school events and recognize student or teacher achievements.

COST-FREE CONSULTING

Individuals outside your school can provide a different point of view, much-
needed expertise, and community connections that will maximize your marketing efforts. Even if someone can participate only on an occasional basis,
the contribution can be significant.

Look among parents, community partners, and volunteers for people with
skills and expertise in marketing, public relations, advertising, graphic design
or other services to help with the school's marketing efforts. Individuals with
marketing, public relations, advertising, or technical expertise can provide
valuable counseling and services. Retired businesspeople have a wealth of
knowledge they can share. Members of marketing-related organizations may
agree to serve as part-time consultants.

As people become involved, they offer access to a larger pool of talent.
If an individual cannot help, maybe she knows someone who can. Ask external partners if they know someone from a company or organization who
would volunteer some time. If there are universities or art institutes in your
area, check with the art, communication, or marketing departments. Gradu-
ate students may be willing to accept a project or internship for little or no
money. Solicit help through an article about the marketing effort in the school
newsletter or even a neighborhood paper.

Set up communication channels so that all external individuals involved
in a project know and communicate with each other and the marketing team.
Marketing team members should feel that volunteers are there to help them
not take over the project. Conversely, volunteers want to feel that they are a
part of the team, not just doing menial tasks.

Including a member from an important demographic or ethnic group within
your community can benefit communication and outreach initiatives. If older
people make up a significant portion of the community, try to recruit a retired
individual who is active in the community as a volunteer consultant.

Be considerate of the volunteers' time. They are there to serve as advisors,
not work as employees.

SET OUT THE WELCOME MAT FOR COMMUNITY GROUPS

Making school facilities available for community meetings and sports activities is a way to acquaint local residents with your school and to express a willingness to reach out to all members of the community. It is also a good way to show off the school's achievements.

Allowing classrooms to be used for meetings provides an opportunity to display the school's level of learning and teaching to those who may not otherwise be aware of it. Set up displays of student projects and accomplishments where visitors can see them. Have information about the school readily available.

Check with the district's legal staff to ensure that the school is protected from any liability. Provide groups who wish to use school facilities with district rules and regulations, release of liability forms, and activity restrictions in written form and have them sign any required forms before allowing use of school property.

GOOD FRIENDS TO HAVE

Realtors, developers, and apartment complex managers can be some of the best friends a school has. Equally, the school can be a good friend to them. Good schools are one reason why people move into a certain area. Get to know the realtors and builders in your area, have them visit the school, and include them in partner activities.

- Provide realtors and developers with school brochures to include in their sales materials.
- Offer school tours to prospective buyers.
- Put homebuyers' names and addresses in the marketing database.
- Ask realty companies, developers, and apartment complexes to put a link to the school's website on their websites.
- Invite realtors to make presentations such as "Buying Your First Home" or "Selling in a Buyers' Market" to parents' events at the school.
- Ask apartment complexes to include school information in new-tenant packets and distribute bulletins to present residents.
- Send notices of school events to apartment complexes for posting on the their bulletin board.

In addition to student-related information, include details about volunteer programs, adult classes, and sports and other events that may be of interest to retirees and single tenants.

RECOGNIZING SPECIAL DATES

Special education dates (National Teachers Day and American Education Week) are occasions for community partners to recognize, in a public and supportive way, the contributions of public education and the dedication and accomplishments of teachers. Partners can put posters or exhibits in their businesses, write articles for the local papers in support of public education, and put a "thank you" to teachers on a marquee.

Retail partners (stores, movie theaters, car washes, etc.) can give teachers a special discount on National Teachers Day. Promotions of this kind benefit businesses by bringing in new customers and creating loyalty among existing ones.

A DAILY REMINDER

Collaborate with business partners to produce a "we support our schools" calendar. Businesses that traditionally give out calendars such as banks, auto dealers, insurance agencies, and printing companies are likely partners. Do not forget local photographic studios; they are a natural partner for this type of promotion.

Sell your partners on the idea by suggesting that calendars with pictures of local school students and activities may be more appealing to customers, especially parents, than the usual pictures of scenery and small animals. The calendar promotes the school within the community and serves as a daily reminder that the business is a school supporter.

The calendar can have a composite of school pictures or a theme such as fine arts activities or new programs in the school. The quality and composition of pictures should be of professional quality. Make sure that photographs taken for inclusion comply with production specifications for high-quality images. And, as with all photographs of students, obtain parents' consent.

NIGHT SCHOOL

Classes at night or on the weekend are a way to reach community residents who do and do not have children in school. When they come for classes, the people in the community are developing an association with the school.

Parents and community residents of limited English proficiency are often reluctant to participate in or even visit the school because they feel unable to communicate effectively. Offering classes in English is a good way to engage them with the school. Language classes provide a more comfortable environment for parents to interact with teachers and staff members. As parents become more comfortable coming to the school, they may participate more in other activities that include their children.

Individuals within the community may be willing to provide classes on cooking or exercise for a small participant fee if the school provides the classrooms. The school's business partners may offer classes as a way to promote themselves. A local nursery can provide a class on gardening tips. A computer store can offer tips on buying computer hardware and software. A hardware store can hold classes on repair and improvement projects. A local medical center or hospital may present classes or information seminars on health-related issues. A real estate company can give a seminar on how to buy or sell a home and the bank can guide participants through the loan process.

Clarify with participating businesses that this is not a venue for hard selling. The primary goal is to offer a service to the community. If the presentation is beneficial, attendees will have a favorable impression of the business providers. People will not come if they feel they will be subjected to a sales pitch.

Meaningful programs at the school benefit everyone involved. Participants receive useful information and training, business partners have access to new customers in positive, helpful environment, and the school is seen as caring, community partner.

MAKING THE MOST OF COMMUNITY EVENTS

Community fairs, holiday events, and parades are occasions for the school to interact with many different groups within the community. Events are opportunities to meet people who are not likely to know about the school other than through the media or neighbors. Set up an information booth at community events, march in the Fourth of July parade or provide a marching band, or build a school float for the neighborhood parade.

The school can join with other schools in the area to organize a community-wide fair that showcases the local schools and their supporters. This is also an occasion to highlight how partners' contributions are making a difference at the school. Your partners will love this kind of public recognition.

The ideas in this chapter can go a long way toward establishing good internal and external relations. Good relations with employees, parents, and the community can make your job much easier as an administrator. Incorporate as many as possible into the marketing initiative. Ask other schools what they are doing to improve public relations. Share your successes with them. Use the Internet to find new ideas. Remember, for a little effort, the rewards can be great.

Chapter 5

Fund-Raising

Cash-strapped districts and schools across the country are looking for ways to meet their budgets. Decreases in state funding and increases in legislative mandates have caused schools to eliminate many of the programs that provide students with an enriched learning environment. Some schools maintain programs by charging fees. Unfortunately, the students who can benefit most from these programs are often the ones least able to pay extra fees. Other schools look to parents, employees, and the community to provide the basic needs of schools such as cleaning supplies and classroom equipment. Schools also need funds for things for which they cannot spend state or federal dollars. As a consequence of the increasing need to generate additional income, school fund-raisers have become an accepted, if not always welcome, part of the school year for both schools and parents.

At a time when schools are scrambling for money, however, many of the traditional sources of income are meeting resistance from parents, educational organizations, and legislatures. Income from vending machines in schools has been drastically reduced as bans on soft drinks, candy, and high-calorie snacks are enforced for health reasons.

Tragic incidents have shown door-to-door selling of products such a candy, candles, wrapping paper, cookie dough, popcorn, and magazines to be dangerous and several districts have banned them. Consequently, parents feel an obligation to buy products they do not want, do not need, and often cannot afford in order to avoid door-to-door sales. Teachers and school staff members must spend time away from their work activities to unpack boxes, hand out products, track sales, and collect money. In return for their efforts, the school gets to keep about half of the money received. Most parents and school employees will tell you they would welcome a reduction in product sales.

Districts as well as schools are looking for new ways to fund initiatives and meet their basic needs. In this chapter, I discuss some of the current, new approaches to fund-raising and offer questions to pose as your district or school considers them.

Naming rights and corporate sponsorships and donations have become so popular that some districts have created administrative positions dedicated to finding sponsors and negotiating contracts with them. Seminars are available to show administrators how to maximize their ability to generate revenue from corporate sponsorships. Critics feel it is slapping a "For Sale" sign on education.

Advertising is going beyond book covers and scoreboards. All sorts of companies are eager to pitch their products to students in an increasing number of ways. School administrators struggle with their need for revenue and the effects of advertising on young minds.

Traditional fund-raising that relies on parent purchases is still the norm in most schools. Corporations are beginning to see the schools' efforts to raise money as a new marketing opportunity. Opportunities and pitfalls exist for both schools and companies as they explore how to get beyond popcorn and candy bars.

NAMING RIGHTS AND CORPORATE SPONSORSHIPS

Following the trend set by professional sports teams, school districts have begun to take advantage of corporations' willingness to pay to get their names in front of students, parents, and the public. Facilities that used to be named for local heroes, distinguished citizens, or the philanthropists who donated money for their construction are today as likely to be named for the corporations who purchase the right to have their name associated with them. For a negotiated sum, companies have the opportunity to have their name heard every time the facility is mentioned, extensive signage, and exclusive rights.

Companies may also contribute electronic systems, equipment, supplies, and clothing, which give them additional exposure and can build product awareness among the students who use them. In addition to marketing and public relations benefits, companies report that they see sponsorships as a way to attract students not only as customers but as future employees.

Some parents, even the community at large, express concern that district administrators will extend naming rights beyond public usage facilities such as stadiums and performance halls to include schools. They argue that the traditional practice of naming schools and administrative buildings after historical and national figures, philanthropists, or local individuals who played a role in advancing education is a way to honor those contributions and provide role models for students. The idea that having a corporate name associated with a school is a right that can be purchased rather than an honor that is earned is distasteful to many. "What next?" a parent asks, "Are we going to have Miller's Roofing and Siding Elementary School? This isn't corporate philanthropy, it's corporate advertising."

An alternative to the outright naming of schools is to allow areas of the school to be open for sponsorship. Playgrounds, gymnasiums, auditoriums, libraries, and instructional areas may be sponsored by appropriate companies. An engineering firm or chemical company might sponsor a science lab or office supply store refurbish the library.

Some critics see corporate naming rights as taxpayer-funded advertising when a company pays $100,000 to have $3 million public-funded stadium named after it. In their eagerness for funds, district may not negotiate the best deal. Remember, you can't rename the stadium every year. A $100,000 may look attractive, but if the term is for ten years, that is only $10,000 per year. As one superintendent commented, "I don't regret selling the naming rights to the stadium, I regret selling them too cheaply."

Naming rights and sponsorships can offset the costs of maintaining and improving facilities, but decisions should be made carefully to avoid unintended consequences. Below are some considerations regarding decisions and agreements for naming rights and sponsorships:

- Obviously companies that sell alcohol and tobacco are taboo, but what about companies that may be seen as polluters, have labor relations issues, have an association with defective or unhealthy products, are involved in major litigation, or are in an unstable financial situation? These issues may result in embarrassment, public relations problems, and financial consequences. In 2001, when Enron Corporation spiraled down in corporate disgrace, the Houston Astros wanted Enron's name removed from their baseball stadium. Enron forced the Astros to buy back the naming rights before they could remove the name. This may be a rare, unanticipated occurrence; however, it would be wise to consider public opinion in your choice and do research on the potential sponsor's history.

- If the company expects exclusivity, how will this affect other revenue sources? For example, a soft drink sponsor stipulates that only its products can be sold at events in the facility. Will this affect other sponsorships? How will it affect them? How will attendees react if they cannot buy beverages other than the sponsors? Will attendees be prohibited from bringing a competitor's products into the facility?
- Does the sponsor expect rights to additional areas or structures such as field houses, parking lots, or concession stands? Can rights to these facilities be sold to other sponsors?
- What happens if competitors of the sponsoring company want to hold events in the facility? For example, Bank A has the naming rights to the stadium. For years, Bank B has paid the school to hold a popular charity fund-raising event in the stadium. Will the district have to forego hosting such events? If so, will the potential loss of such events have a significant negative impact?
- What happens if the company goes out of business, merges, or is bought out by another company? If buyout or merger involves a name change, who has the financial responsibility for making changes to signage? Do rights convey to the new company? What happens if the products or services of the buyout company conflict with district policy of sponsorships? What are the termination rights and responsibilities of both parties? During the recent economic downturn, as businesses went into bankruptcy, some districts lost their sponsors for large, newly installed electronic scoreboards. Does the district have contingency plans for such circumstances?
- Is the company willing to include other forms of contributions such as equipment, clothing, and supplies? If not, will other companies be allowed to do so?
- Some of the concern with naming and sponsorships is not that it is being done, but how. Have a clear understanding with the sponsor of what any signage will look like and how prevalent it will be. The district should have the right to review and approve signage and promotional products. A gaudy, rotating, blazing neon sign is sure to generate complaints. People are accustomed to seeing plaques, lettering over entryways, and other forms of recognition at public buildings, and they are not as likely to object when school sponsorships are kept within such boundaries.

ADVERTISING

Advertising has been in schools for generations. Remember the advertisement for the local car dealer at football field and the book covers, pencils, bookmarks, and pens during your school days? What has changed today is the scope of advertising. Today, as companies realize the purchasing power and buying influence of school children, advertising has become a lot more prevalent and a lot more lucrative. School districts in need of extra dollars are eager to consider their proposals.

Advertising is popping up just about anywhere there is space: cafeterias, hallways, even restrooms. A district located near the landing path for the Dallas/Fort Worth International airport offered advertising space on its school roofs.

Several state legislatures have cleared the way for advertising on the inside and outside of buses. The type of advertising and its size and placement are generally regulated. If your district decides to pursue putting ads on buses, I recommend hiring an advertising company with expertise in this type of advertising. These companies already have a client base of advertisers and experience in negotiating contracts. The company should provide you with earnings projections, anticipated costs, a list of potential advertisers, and the names of their school district clients.

The district's agreement with the advertising company should specify the following: the fees charged to advertisers; who has the financial responsibility for design, production, installation, maintenance, removal, and replacement of signage; what types of products are not allowed; the size of signs; how they are attached and where; how revenues are shared; and who has the responsibility for signs that are vandalized, damaged, or become unsightly.

A question that often arises is whether the advertising is placed inside as well as outside of buses. Some may not object to outside advertising that the public occasionally sees, but oppose advertising inside that is targeted toward a captive audience of students who see it every day. If the district chooses to allow ads inside, it may want a stricter code for what can be advertised to students. A group including a board member, district or school administrator, and a parent should review and approve all advertising before it is attached to buses. It is advisable to call some of the districts on the company's client list. Their experiences and recommendations can be valuable.

In-school advertising can be placed anywhere in the school where there is a place for it. The question is, should it? Parents express the view that children are bombarded with advertising everywhere these days. Schools should be a respite from ubiquitous commercialism. The counterargument is that advertising is so prevalent that children are used to it and the impact is minimal.

One of the more controversial forms of in-school advertising is the use of a daily news program to get a couple of minutes of age-appropriate advertising in front of students. Critics argue that because the advertising is coming to the students through the school, by association it has more credibility and influence especially among younger students and those in high-poverty areas. Again, there is the objection to students being a captive audience. Parents and education groups argue that if schools are allowing advertising, then part of the curriculum should educate children to critically assess the commercials they see and hear to distinguish manipulation, hype, and hidden messages.

A less controversial form of advertising is one that individuals see or hear by choice. Recently, a large urban district entered into an agreement with a private media company to create a new Internet-based radio station which is expected to generate more than $500,000 a year for the district. Listeners can access the station through the district's website, a link through a local TV channel site, or an iPhone application. Music will be the main content; however, the station also will provide information on district and school events, performances, and news items. Students will play a role in creating the content. Approximately five minutes of advertising per hour will target the districts employees and families; however, products such as tobacco, alcohol, and junk food are prohibited.

In addition to the evident forms of advertising mentioned above, a more subtle form known as embedded advertising or product placement is making its way into classrooms. Many parents find this form of advertising even more objectionable.

When James Bond checks his Omega watch as he races around in his BMW or when the hip, successful women on the latest "hot" TV program chat about their designer shoes and handbags as they type on their Sony laptops and chat on iPhones, advertisers are sending you a message—these "cool" people love these products, you will too. These covert messages are becoming more widespread as advertisers try to reach consumers who tune out traditional commercials. Companies see product placements as a way to create product awareness, build brand loyalty, and influence how we view certain issues and industries.

This type of advertising comes to the classroom through the books, DVDs, lesson plans, posters, games, and other materials that companies supply free to teachers through websites, direct mailing, conferences, and corporate-sponsored teaching workshops. Some advertising make use of photos and repetition of the brand name in materials. A mathematics exercise asks students to figure out how to evenly divide a (name brand) pizza, use (name brand) pieces of chocolate in counting tens, or figure out how long it will take two (name brand) cars traveling at different speeds to meet at a particular point. Students receive coloring books with pictures featuring a particular restaurant chain, theme park, or cartoon characters.

Companies may also use materials to create a desired image or influence perceptions. It may be difficult to determine if the information in these materials is biased or distorted, especially if the source for data used to substantiate viewpoints is not revealed. Students read a book about the history of energy production in which certain industries are portrayed in a more favorable way than others. A science lesson describes the advantages of certain methods of food production without mentioning differing opinions concerning adverse effects and negative costs/benefits.

It is understandable that teachers are eager to obtain supplemental materials the school cannot afford. Generally, however, these materials are obtained directly by teachers and are not subject to any kind of review process. Administrators need to establish a set of guidelines for evaluating materials. There is information available on the Internet to help schools establish criteria for what is acceptable in the classroom. Some general questions are as follows: Who produced the data? Who paid for the study? Are differing viewpoints discussed impartially? Are certain facts and events ignored? Is there an obvious bias? Are design elements used to create specific perceptions? Are absolutes such as *all, every, never,* and *always* used. What sociological, political, economic, or cultural attitudes are indirectly reflected in the advertisement?

Teachers can use materials for competing viewpoints in student debates. This helps students critically analyze how the arguments were constructed. Students should be taught to evaluate advertising messages to detect exaggeration, manipulations, distortions, and out-and-out deception. Are famous or authoritative figures used to promote the message? Do these people have credibility? Why should we find them credible? Advertising is not going to disappear. Its pervasiveness and influence can be limited.

Fund-raising at the school level is still predominately done through the selling of products to parents. Corporations previously not involved in such sales are beginning to see this as a marketing opportunity. Restaurants, retail chains, and even some service providers are trying various programs to get people into their places of businesses as a way to raise money for schools. Schools should examine these programs carefully and have realistic expectations about parent participation and how much money can be raised.

Below are some factors to consider before signing on for a fund-raising program:

- Have a contract and make sure it clearly defines the responsibilities of the school and of the partner company regarding activities related to equipment, materials, and activities used to promote the program in the community; the school's right to review and approve content of promotional material; who has financial responsibility for promotional materials and activities; the length of the program; school's percentage of profit and whether the percentage is based on gross or net income; when and how will funds earned by school be distributed; termination rights of the school; and the school's protection from legal action.

- Determine whether the program is appropriate for the community. If the program requires that people take action online, do most members of the community have Internet access? If the program requires that people shop at certain stores or eat at certain restaurants, are these the kind of places your community patronizes? How frequently? If the program requires that people use credit or debit cards, are these forms of payment your community is likely to use? Are people required to use special program cards, mention the program before purchase, or give a special code they must remember?

- If the school receives a one-time sign-up fee for a service, what happens if a person cancels the service? Is there an early termination fee? Are taxes, upgrade fees, and other charges clearly stated? Does the school have any financial liability in case of cancellation?

- How is this type of fund-raising likely to be viewed by the community? If the program involves forms of advertising, will the community find it objectionable? Are promotional activities likely to be considered acceptable? For example, a promotional activity that rewards only those students who bring in a predetermined level of sales penalizes students who are at a disadvantage in meeting that level.

- What is the return on investment (ROI)? This is not necessarily a monetary investment. How much extra work is the program for schools employees? Are there costs to the school? Is the return worth the school's investment in time and money?

Several years ago, a large urban district came up with a Big Hairy Audacious Goal (BHAG). The goal was to change the face of school fund-raising. The goal was to create a fund-raising program that met the following criteria: involve no selling of unwanted, unneeded products; earn continuous year-round income for schools; relieve teachers and school staff members of time-consuming fund-raising tasks; and be provided at no cost to the school or supporters. The first attempt involved a partnership with a private company. It took two years to negotiate and implement the program and it was not a success. The program ended a few months after it was launched when the private company was bought out and the new company terminated the program. The district did, however, learn some valuable lessons from the experience.

The next attempt was to create and administer the program from within the district. The new program allowed school supporters to earn monthly income for their favorite schools when they use electricity. Participating retail electric providers agreed to offer their lowest available electric rates and pay a monthly contribution to the school the supporter designates when he or she signs up for electricity through the program website. Schools have the potential to earn several hundred dollars a month year round. There is no cost to the school or the supporter to participate. The program is not limited to parents. Relatives, neighbors, alumni, even businesses can participate.

The program had limited success. People were reluctant to change their electric service companies even if it meant money to the school and the opportunity to eliminate traditional fund-raising. There is an odd phenomenon in people and organizations. They will often continue with ineffective programs if change is involved. Innovation is not always welcome. Even welcome innovation may take time to produce the desired outcome.

Although there has been some grumbling from parents and education organizations about the commercialization of education, sponsorships, and advertising, some of the new fund-raising methods are a way for districts and schools to get what they need without requiring extra fees or raising taxes. Whatever the feelings, the need for schools and districts to raise funds will not diminish any time soon. The alternatives are to increase state and federal funding for education or to give our students less of what they need.

Summary

The environment in which schools function will continue to change. Demands for higher standards, greater competition from alternative forms of education, increased need for community support, and challenges in recruiting high-quality personnel require that schools and districts have the methods, materials, and mind-set to be aware of and to meet the needs, wants, and expectations of their internal and external stakeholders. An organized marketing effort will help schools accomplish this.

As stated in the beginning of this book, many schools are already marketing, whether they call it this or not. Often what they lack is a strategy to maximize their efforts. I hope this book will assist schools in initiating, implementing, and maintaining an effective marketing plan to mutually benefit themselves and their communities and thereby enhance the learning experience for all students.

Appendix A

Success Story

John J. Herrera Elementary
Marketing Makes a Difference

John J. Herrera Elementary School, Houston, Texas, is an example of how a well-executed marketing effort can benefit a school's students, staff members, and community.

The level of excellence achieved by the students and staff of John J. Herrera Elementary School contradicts the stereotypical view of its student demographics. The student population is 96 percent Hispanic (45 percent Limited English Proficiency), 95.5 percent Free/Reduced Lunch, 51 percent At-Risk, with a mobility rate of 21 percent. Yet, the school ranks as an Exemplary School, the highest rating granted by the Texas Education Agency (TEA).

In addition to teaching experience and a master of education, Herrera principal Hector Rodríguez has an MBA and several years in private business. His experience in the private sector gives Mr. Rodríguez an appreciation of the power of a well-organized and focused marketing effort.

To Mr. Rodríguez, marketing is not an option. "We have a different environment from past years regarding how we are accountable for what we are doing in our schools. We are also performing in a more competitive and sophisticated environment. To succeed in the type of environment, schools need to have a complete understanding of what they are doing and how they are doing it. Then they need to communicate, and, in some cases, educate their communities about what they are doing. Finally, every school needs to understand how similar and different their services are from those of other schools and learn how to highlight their uniqueness."

"Marketing is not something we do occasionally," stated Mr. Rodríguez, "because marketing is about product improvement, customer satisfaction, and effective communication, and these are things we are always striving toward.

An effective marketing program should come naturally in everything you do within school activities. It is an understanding that the final product is student growth directly and staff and community growth indirectly. A positive culture sells itself!"

Principal Rodríguez knows that no amount of marketing can substitute for an inferior product. The highest marketing and academic priority for administration and staff is creating the best academic products possible. A good product is one that meets the needs and wants of the customer: an outstanding product is one that *exceeds* the customers' needs and wants. The administration and staff dedicate considerable thought to academic programs that not only shape the students' present and future success but also benefit the community at large.

The marketing approach creates an atmosphere in which individuals are always thinking, "How can we create a better product?" At Herrera, the administration and staff continually strive to create a product that is excellent in quality and innovative in its approach to learning. Part of the marketing strategy is to combine the latest technology with inventive programs that continually improve the learning environment. The school is dedicated to finding creative ways for students and teachers to venture beyond the boundaries of textbooks and to search the world electronically for new ideas. This approach has made Herrera a preferred school for students and parents.

One of Herrera's outstanding products is its two-way language immersion program in grades kindergarten through second. Limited English Proficient students and monolingual English students are together in classes where they develop fluency in both languages as well as a strong foundation in academic areas. The ultimate goal is to produce bilingual and biliterate students throughout the school. This type of program is attractive not only to parents, most of whom are Spanish speaking, but also to businesses in a state where being bilingual is a valuable asset.

The school's technology-driven curriculum transcends the standard computer-based learning. One example is the daily morning show transmitted from the school's broadcast center. The show is a means to communicate important information, recognize achievements, encourage confidence and build self-esteem. A typical morning includes comments from the principal, a weather report and the lunch menu delivered by the students, and recognition of student accomplishments and birthdays. The program always closes with the school pledge: "Today, I will respect my teacher, my peers, and my school. I will do more than is expected of me."

The daily broadcast provides more than a means to communicate information within the school. The program helps students to develop technical expertise early in their academic careers while teaching valuable lessons in organization, project management, research, design, and communication.

Students have used the school's technology to address issues important to them and the community. Many of the students have relatives in the military, some serving in Iraq. The school wanted a way to lessen the fears and concerns of the students. Students and faculty created a video that incorporated excerpts from student essays on "Why I Like America" and pictures of relatives in the military with patriotic symbols and music. The video had a significant effect on the students' ability to cope with the uncertainty and apprehension they felt about what they see and hear in the media.

The high-quality programs at Herrera Elementary allow the school to position itself as an organization that takes the community's needs and wants seriously and is meeting them successfully. The ultimate product of Herrera, however, is the student who is enhanced significantly by the quality programs the school provides. From the earliest grade levels, students are acquiring language and technical proficiency that will benefit their lives and the economics of the community.

Explaining his philosophy, Principal Rodríguez said, "Marketing is developing a product or service and its concept. In essence, you understand your product and create a concept around it. For example, at Herrera Elementary, we want to communicate quality education which is based on caring for children, relationships with our community, use of technology, and language development and maintenance, both Spanish and English."

Mr. Rodríguez knows that the environment where the product is delivered is important in marketing. The school's emphasis on using technology to maximize the learning experience is evident. To utilize fully the benefits of the broadcast studio, every classroom has a VideoLAN server, a DVD player, and television monitor. There is one computer for every two students.

Mr. Rodríguez also believes that schools can and must strike a balance between a safe environment and a welcoming one. Schools need to protect their children. At the same time, parents, volunteers, or community partners must feel welcome or they will not participate. At Herrera, the welcome is apparent before the visitor enters the front door. The school grounds are clean and tidy and visitor parking is available at the school entrance. The school interior is immaculate. The staff implements security measures in ways that do not make visitors feel like intruders. The atmosphere is one of high energy and activity with a purpose.

An environment that represents excellence attracts top-notch people. In return, these people are motivated to sustain and cultivate the level of excellence that makes the environment so attractive. The marketing effort at

Herrera is successful in attracting talented people and in utilizing their participation to promote the level of excellence.

All professional staff members are qualified for gifted and talented education. Last year, the school lost none of its quality teachers. Principal Rodríguez attributes the school's ability to recruit and retain quality staff to an internal atmosphere of respect, high standards, and professionalism. The high level of professionalism mixed with a heavy measure of enthusiasm and pride creates an environment that attracts quality people.

The level of achievement and pride exhibited by the school's staff and students also attracts parents. Parents and the community, in general, are eager to be a part of the school's positive atmosphere. The school encourages participation in various ways. Herrera uses traditional methods, which include Volunteers in Public Schools (VIPS), PTA, and an "Open Door" policy for parents; however, it also uses more unconventional methods.

Each year, Herrera hosts its annual Fathers' Night, where between 100 and 150 fathers (and some mothers) attend presentations on school and community issues during a catered dinner. This is an effort to target an important segment of the population that traditionally does not participate in such events. The school makes the evening fun for the fathers, each of whom receives a book to "autograph" and present to his child as a gift. To add special interest, fathers can win door prizes, such as tools and sports equipment.

Another such event is the "Día del Nino" celebration, during which the PTA and community members and business partners come together to celebrate childhood. This event relates to the Mexican tradition of the Día del Nino, celebrated every year on April 30.

The school holds celebrations, often featuring traditional Mexican Mariachi music, throughout the year to recognize achievements. After the state-mandated test, the school celebrates with a carnival for the children. A Mothers' Day celebration recognizes mothers and provides certificates of appreciation to the school's VIPS.

The school conducts weekly parenting sessions that address community and family issues, as well as developmental considerations for fifth graders moving on to middle school. When needed, teachers bring parents into classrooms to sit with their children to help them establish long-term goals and evaluate their children's academic and behavioral performance.

Another annual event, which takes place after the beginning of the school year, is a field trip for parents and their children to the Museum of Health. This event involves parents in their children's learning, introduces parents and students to the museum, and increases parents' awareness of health issues concerning their children and themselves.

The after-school program at Herrera is designed to assist the working parent. Students remain in school under supervision until 5:30 p.m., when parents can collect their children. The children experience enrichment activities, both academic and cultural. This has become a critical program in the development of strong relationships with those working parents.

The school creates an awareness of its presence in the community by participating in community parades and other civic events. School tours are scheduled on Friday mornings from January to May, a time when parents are most likely to be selecting a school for the next year.

Herrera has developed strong relationships with many community partners, including the City of Houston, Museum of Fine Arts, YMCA, police and fire departments, and the neighborhood Fiesta food market, who help with children's festivals and other events. Partners donate items as door prizes for the Fathers' Night or become involved as guest speakers for career days and/or Fathers' Night.

In other situations, organizations have helped by awarding grants for special projects, such as the YES Grant ($2,000 for use in purchasing safety equipment) and the Houston Rocket's $1,000 grant for field trips for kindergarten students. Herrera has enjoyed the Harris County grant, which has provided more than $200,000 for after-school program over the past several years, and the Capital Investment grant, which provides over $40,000 to spend with parents and teachers.

Many parents who have skills in the crafts have donated their time and resources to the school. Some of these relationships have resulted in donations for faculty luncheons or holiday celebrations. The participation of individuals, businesses, and organizations from the community creates an encouraging climate within the school.

Mr. Rodríguez expresses the importance of involving everyone in the marketing effort when he says, "Our teachers and our parents are our best salespeople." Their commitment and participation are powerful testimonials.

Mr. Rodríguez is aware that everything, even the smallest thing, about the school creates an impression and communicates a message. "Simply, we want everyone to know what sets Herrera Elementary apart from the crowd: what make us different and unique." The school uses a number of mediums to create an awareness of the school and its accomplishments.

The school uniform is a polo-type shirt or t-shirt with the Herrera Elementary School logo and "We ♥ Our Children" on the front. On one sleeve is printed "Exemplary School 2002–2003." The uniform is a tangible, public announcement of the school's pride in its accomplishments. In addition to being an "advertisement" for the high quality of the school, the uniform creates a sense of belonging and special membership among the students. In turn, students are more likely to give extra effort toward maintaining the excellence of the school and their place in it.

The school brochure is a simple, concise, and straightforward expression of the school's achievements, programs, and mission. In addition to a photograph of the school, the cover lists the school's academic standing since 1995. The first thing the reader sees is a clear, objective affirmation of the school's commitment to excellence. The brochure text communicates the school's emphasis on excellence, technology, and foreign language development and provides information such as educational strategies and programs and a profile of teacher demographics.

The website reaches out to the community by going beyond supplying school information that students and parents want to know. It draws parents to the site by providing links to valuable information that can help families in their daily lives. Herrera has recently developed a school DVD that highlights much of the spirit and programs at Herrera Elementary. This DVD is used for special guests and visitors, or specific groups with interest in the school. The school will use this technique to target potential business partners (in marketing terms, "selected segments" of interest to our school).

The community around Herrera Elementary is not wealthy, but Rodríguez believes that the community deserves a level of education and resulting student achievement equal to schools in more affluent neighborhoods. Principal Rodríguez and the staff members at Herrera Elementary are delivering a product that is of the highest quality. In return, the community gives value back to the school. The community pays taxes, but value does not always involve money. A high level of parental involvement and community support adds value that helps the school maintain a high level of quality. The community, in turn, believes it is receiving value for the price it pays in taxes, contributions of time and money, and support of the school's goals. A price the community pays willingly.

Appendix B

Success Story

Colorado Springs School District 11

Electronic Dialogue: A Means to Greater Community Loyalty

With over 30,000 students, School District 11 is the seventh largest school district in Colorado and the largest school district in the Pikes Peak region. The district includes 38 elementary schools (grades K–5); 1 K–8 school; 9 middle schools (grades 6–8); 5 high schools (grades 9–12); 5 alternative schools and/or programs; 1 digital high school; 6 charter schools; and adult and family education programs. Nestled at the foot of Pikes Peak and the front range of the Colorado Rockies, Colorado Springs, with a population of about 400,000, would appear to be an idyllic location in which to raise and educate children; and it is.

However, District 11 faced challenges related to the inner-city characteristics of the area that it serves, which is the older, more established part of the city. Many of the people in District 11's community are retired or no longer have school-age children, giving them less motivation to vote for additional taxes or mill levies in support of District 11.

Suburban expansion had hit Colorado Springs, like most cities, resulting in many of the more affluent families moving away from the center of the city into school districts which now surround District 11. This had limited the district's ability to expand its service area and reintegrate some of these newer neighborhoods. This kept the district from being able to expand its taxable base, while the property values have tended to trail the rate of growth of suburban school districts. In addition, as the oldest school district in the Colorado Springs area, District 11 had some of the oldest schools and facilities, which require a lot of maintenance and upkeep and, in many instances, replacement.

Even with these fiscal constraints, District 11 provided a high quality of educational services to its community and had been recognized for its efforts and results in implementing quality and continuous improvement systems. The challenges faced by the district, however, related in many ways to how the district and its educational services and staff members were perceived by the parents and taxpayers of the community.

By the Spring of 2002, District 11 had already deployed numerous online programs to help the district administration and individual campuses interact with the community more effectively. These include a library search system (SIRSI) for finding and reserving library resources throughout the district; a school lunch system to allow students and parents to purchase school lunches online; a community education enrollment system; Teacher Connect, Parent Connect, and Student Connect, which allowed these stakeholders to monitor, collaborate, and seek answers regarding individual class curriculum and assignments as well as information about individual students.

While many of these applications were part of an overall community relations effort using the Internet, the district was only beginning to look at online tools for marketing and customer service functions at the district level. In early 2002, the communications function was receiving proportionally greater emphasis because of the failure earlier in the decade to pass a bond issue which would have helped the district upgrade many of its older facilities.

District 11 had an active communications and community relations office headed by Ms. Elaine Naleski, and the district website contained a broad range of policy and procedural content and went several levels deep with "sub-webs" for different departments within the district. In addition, the site provided links to many of the operational systems mentioned above.

However, the District 11 Communications and Community Relations Office was only beginning to look at ways to streamline their own communication processes and use the Web more interactively to improve responsiveness to the community. As part of her effort to convince the Board of Education to take action regarding an online community relations system, Ms. Naleski identified several benefits, including faster, more efficient, and more convenient delivery of information; customer friendliness (24-hour-a-day availability); quality (e.g., accuracy) of information; the ability to "push out" important information; the ability to track data within the system; and the need to track opinions of the community through online surveying.

Ms. Naleski made a persuasive argument, but there were still concerns about utilizing the Internet for community relations programs, primarily based on a Board of Education perception that it might be seen as less personal than other channels. In the end, Ms. Naleski was able to overcome these concerns because everyone acknowledged the need to take some action to improve the community relations program. From a financial perspective, hiring more staff members to handle these programs was not cost-effective; therefore, after almost a year of internal discussion and review, the board gave the D-11 Communications Office the go-ahead to find an Internet-based community relations tool.

One of the first processes identified for improvement was the e-mail system that came through the district's website. There were several links on the site where users could click and send an e-mail to the district. The vast majority of these e-mails landed in the inbox of one person in the District 11 Communications Office, who then had to track down the answers from a knowledgeable person or department and respond to the users. This process resulted in a relatively long response time, redundant responses to the same questions, and a procedural bottleneck because questions could be processed only as fast as one person could track down the answers.

To address this bottleneck, the District 11 Communications Office decided to develop an online, automated program called "D-11 Answers," which would provide a knowledgebase of frequently asked questions (FAQs) on their website. The system would also direct questions to the correct person or department within the district most likely to know the answers, automatically updating the knowledgebase with the answers once staff responded. In addition, the D-11 Communications Office needed a way to track response time and unanswered questions.

When considering options for the system, Ms. Naleski's team had to decide whether to wait on the information technology (IT) department to develop such a program or go outside for assistance. After much internal discussion, it was decided to go with an outside system. Since the D-11 Communications Office did not want the project to depend on availability of IT resources to install a commercial system on the district's own servers, they chose a hosted solution. The hosted system, called "ezCommunicator," had the knowledge base function and also included several other interactive components. The D-11 Communications Office could have chosen a system that had only knowledge base functions, but they recognized that they would probably want to expand to use of other online interactive components. Having those components available in a single integrated system made it easier to deploy these other functions on an as-needed basis.

"One of the first and largest challenges we faced was getting buy-in from the rest of the departments within the district office once we had board approval to proceed with the project," explained Elaine Naleski. Aside from getting IT commitment to the technical side of the D-11 Answers system, the D-11 Communications Office had to persuade, and in some cases cajole, different departments to take on responsibility for responding to questions in their areas of expertise.

With D-11 Answers deployed, the D-11 Communications Office has been able to track the trend in usage of the system, both for viewing questions and posting questions. They have also, from a quality improvement aspect, been able to track the response time to questions coming through the system and have seen a steady improvement to a level of approximately one business day, which was an original target for quality.

Since November 2003, when the above information was compiled and presented at an international education conference, District 11 has continued to expand their use of the Internet as part of their communications and community relations programs.

In early 2004, the District 11 administration was beginning to search for ways to market particular high schools within the district that were losing students and suffering from poor community perception. As part of the community outreach and marketing efforts at these high schools, the D-11 Communications Office decided to deploy the same system used at the district level on the school websites so that these schools can begin to utilize more interactive, Internet-based tools to strengthen community loyalty.

The D-11 Communications Office has gradually broadened use of the interactive tools within the ezCommunicator system and now distributes electronic newsletters to various subscribers of the system. They use the survey and online poll capabilities to gain quick insights into community interest and positions on certain issues, and they provide users with the opportunity to subscribe to various announcement groups and categories of interest.

In November 2004, District 11 ran another bond election and was successful in getting voter approval for $132 million for capital improvements across the district. While many people were involved and many other methods were used to get out the message about the value of the bond to the community, District 11 was able to make effective use of their D-11 Answers system to respond to questions submitted by the voters in the community and to take periodic surveys and polls to gauge support.

"We've learned that we could have gained more benefit earlier in using the system if we had planned out how we would apply each of the features to its fullest effect. We also learned that we should have involved more people, including end users, in the process of defining our requirements in order to get their buy-in up-front," said Ms. Naleski. "Using the Internet as part of our communications strategy is a process of continuous advancement. We're always looking for ways to use the Website and e-mail to refine our message to the community and improve the community's perception of us as a responsive school district committed to the highest level of quality education. Implementing an Internet community relations system has been, and continues to be, a journey for us—not a single event."

Appendix C

Success Story

Community Connections for All Students/Arts Education Matters

As part of their effort to benefit their city, a major Houston philanthropic organization, the Robert and Janice McNair Foundation, approached the Houston Heights Association and Houston Independent School District's then North Central District with an offer to establish a partnership designed to improve the quality of life in the historic Heights neighborhood, located five miles northwest of downtown Houston. The resulting agreement, "Community Connections for all Students," began a three-year partnership in which the McNair Foundation pledged $1.5 million to improve school fine arts programs and invest in adult and parent education programs, technology and health education and to generally improve the quality of life in the community. Through a close collaboration between Joanie Haley, McNair Foundation Executive Director, and Heights resident Jerri Workman of the Greater Heights Education Partnership, "Community Connections" became a model in collaborative initiatives so successful that the McNair Foundation chose to continue its support beyond the original three-year commitment.

A major goal for the school fine arts program component was to create an initiative funded by the McNair Foundation that would have the greatest possible impact on arts education by facilitating partnerships between Houston-area arts organizations and inner-city public schools. At the time, the need was great. A variety of factors, mainly financial, had resulted in the elimination of some fine arts teaching positions and reductions in many fine arts program budgets. Six elementary schools, which served approximately 1,500 students, had no fine arts programs at all. Of those elementary schools that did offer fine arts classes, instruction was available for only 40–50 minutes once a week. As a result, arts programs on the secondary level were few or nonexistent. There was little opportunity for students to experience the fine arts on a meaningful level.

In addition to providing program support, the McNair Foundation also provided matching funds to establish a Coordinator of Fine Arts position to oversee all aspects of the initiative. After an extensive candidate search, R. Neal Wiley was hired as coordinator. Mr. Wiley had 25 years of experience as a fine arts educator in public schools, both as an instructor and as an administrator. He served on the board of directors of Chrysalis Dance Company, InterActive Theater, and Mercury Baroque Ensemble, was on the Education Committee of Young Audiences of Houston, and served as a member of Houston Community College-Central's Visual and Performing Arts Committee. Mr. Wiley was also a consultant to several local and state fine arts organizations. These credentials provided the expertise and contacts to establish a successful program within the original allotted time frame of three years. The program began with 5 Houston-area arts partner organizations providing programs to schools and grew to include 15 arts and education organizations in all fine arts disciplines.

Mr. Wiley knew with a limited amount of time and money, he had to get the most bang for the bucks he had. It was important early on to convey to teachers, administrators, and parents the many benefits of arts programs. Of utmost importance were recent studies indicating that when students have access to fine arts programs, learning is enhanced and achievement is increased. For students who become active in the arts, the development of patience, persistence, discipline, and a sense of accomplishment are benefits that will serve them throughout their lives.

Mr. Wiley had firsthand knowledge of how exposure to things new and wonderful can affect a child's world. "When we go to Jones Hall (Houston's symphony hall), I always try to run ahead of the children, so I can see the expressions on their faces when they come into the hall's spacious entry," explained Mr. Wiley. "Their looks of wonder and surprise tell you that something exceptional is happening. And our teachers report that learning that one must be very quiet in the symphony hall or during a theatrical performance has resulted in positive behavior modification in the classroom."

Activities in the first phase were also devoted to getting schools and parents more actively involved. To get schools involved, program logistics had to be easy. Mr. Wiley knew that a program involving a complicated process or continual effort would not be well received. At the beginning of each school year, a presentation was made to all principals and each one received a fine arts packet describing the activities participating arts organizations were willing to provide. One request form listed *all* activities. Principals simply checked off the activities they wanted for the year. All bookings and communication went through Mr. Wiley's office. In some cases, the schools provided the transportation and the organizations provided the program. In other instances, organizations brought their programs to the school. "I have yet to encounter a principal who did not value fine arts and want the arts in their school," said Mr. Wiley. "Their frustration, and mine, was how to pay for arts programs in the face of declining budgets and in the current atmosphere of high-stakes testing. The approach we have taken, one of collaboration and thinking outside the proverbial box, has taken some time to implement, but the results are undeniable."

Getting the parents' support for the project required overcoming cultural, financial, and logistical challenges to fine arts participation. Mr. Wiley felt the best way to communicate with parents was direct involvement through an arts event. "School events, such as PTA/O programs involving students, are a good way to attract parents to the school," says Mr. Wiley. Parents were also invited to be chaperones on fine arts field trips. In addition to these initiatives, it was decided that an annual community-based signature arts event be held to bring schools and community members together for a special day of fine arts activities.

As a result, an annual Festival of the arts was established and held each spring on the John H. Reagan High School campus. Funded by the McNair Foundation, the Houston Heights Association, and several other local businesses and civic groups, the first festival attracted over 1,000 people. Parents who had never come to the school before were there. The festival, which showcased hundreds of student visual and performing arts experiences, also included representatives of the local fine arts community, giving the event an added level of significance. Attendance and participation increased steadily every year thereafter, and plans were made to hold additional festivals at the other high schools within Houston ISD's Northwest District.

Since the project began, over 350 campus-based student education and outreach programs have been presented. Over 6,000 students have attended performances at the Alley Theatre and in Jones Hall in downtown Houston. Approximately 30 campus-based artist-in-residence programs have been created for area schools, both during the regular instructional day and in after-school programs. The residencies allow artists from the arts partner organizations to work with students on specific projects over a greater period of time, typically several weeks to an entire school year, thereby providing opportunities for students to experience the arts at a depth and complexity previously unavailable to them.

"We're moving away from the 'one-shot' arts experience," explained Mr. Wiley. "We, of course, value individual performances, and we are constantly developing and improving collaboratively-designed integrated lesson plans, pre- and post-performance activities for students, etc., that both enhance the arts experiences as well as tie the experiences to other subject areas. We find that teachers and principals appreciate this a great deal."

Over 150 teachers have been trained in art integration techniques. Foundation donations have been leveraged to bring in approximately $40,000 in additional funds from state and county organizations. By the end of the third year, "Community Connections" was a resounding success, and discussions were initiated to explore ways to expand and replicate the model in other Houston ISD schools.

In a time when diminishing resources were forcing schools to cut back or eliminate their fine arts programs, Joe Nuber, superintendent of the Northwest Administrative District (NWD) in Houston, was determined to maintain an arts presence in the 26 Title I schools in his district, which served some 19,000 economically disadvantaged inner-city children. With plans to expand the original 16 school fine arts initiative to the entire NWD, Mr. Nuber made the bold step of establishing a director of Fine Arts position for the Northwest District, and chose Mr. Wiley to continue to implement and expand to scale the established programs. A key factor in expansion was to secure the continued support of the McNair Foundation.

A bilingual parent survey and a campus principal needs assessment were prepared by the NWD Fine Arts Department and administered to determine levels of need and interest. The bilingual parent survey was administered by participating elementary schools and measured the interest in each fine arts discipline—art, dance, music, and theater. The needs assessment done by NWD principals asked them to project their anticipated fine arts course offerings for the coming academic years, as well as to identify areas of weakness or need in fine arts course offerings. Cumulative results of both the parent interest survey and the principal needs assessment indicated overwhelming support and a clear need for arts education programs in NWD schools beyond what the schools alone could provide.

In response to these survey and needs assessment results, not only did the McNair Foundation continue to support the collaborative fine arts model program, it *increased* the level of support for the second phase of the program. This second phase was called "Arts Education Matters," a groundbreaking and comprehensive program to incrementally integrate arts education into other core subject areas and daily activities in all of the 26 schools in the

NWD over the next five years. Schools were expected to fund a gradually increasing percentage of the overall cost of programs on their campus. Local businesses were sought as collaborative partners with NWD schools to financially support fine arts programs at the schools in their neighborhood. Arts Education Matters (AEM) had four major components:

1. Campus-based **performances** for students, faculty, and staff
2. Campus-based **artist-in-residence** and/or **workshop** experiences
3. **Field trips** to Arts Partners' venues
4. Comprehensive **curriculum integration staff development** experiences for non–fine arts classroom teachers

All four components were a continuation of the original "Community Connections" initiative. AEM's goal was to expand the components to scale in all 26 NWD schools. Additionally, a significant increase in the scope of teacher training through arts curriculum integration staff development opportunities for non–fine arts classroom teachers was a major program component. Without the funds to hire additional fine arts instructors, the goal was to infuse the arts into the schools through non–fine arts teachers.

The first step was AEM's "renewal" process in which teachers were renewed by discovering the wealth of ways in which the arts can have a positive impact upon students' lives and learning. Renewal is an intrinsically motivated approach to self-improvement. Through AEM, educators had the opportunity to learn creative strategies for reaching more students in deep and meaningful ways. Teachers were able to enroll in arts curriculum integration workshops for professional development and gifted and talented credits.

One arts partner in particular, the Museum of Fine Arts, Houston (MFAH), provided the majority of the arts curriculum integration training and also provided follow-up support in the classroom through an art curriculum integration program, *Learning Through Art*. The program was designed by teachers for teachers to show them how to incorporate art instruction into other subjects. Those who completed the training received curriculum kits with integrated lesson plans.

To date, more than 150 teachers have gone through the training and renewal process. The response was so great that participation had to be limited. "The MFAH teacher training program, along with their vast Kinder Teacher Resource Center, has been the single strongest component of our overall fine arts initiative," according to Mr. Wiley. "We view *Learning Through Art* as *the* model for arts integration in public schools."

Mr. Wiley was particularly proud of one approach to showcasing students' artwork—the *Art Space* in the Northwest District's administration building, a permanent gallery installation created with help from the Museum of Fine Arts, Houston. Through the use of special framing, lighting, and small plaques with artwork titles and student artist's name, *Art Space* displayed selected pieces of children's art as though it were in a museum setting.

Mr. Wiley understood that organizations that donate time and money want to see results. To provide independent assessment, Dr. Cynthia Herbert, based in Austin, Texas, served as program evaluator. Formerly executive director of the Texas Alliance for Education and the Arts, which was the Texas member of the Kennedy Center Alliance for Arts Education Network, Dr. Herbert had over 30 years of experience in arts education and was considered an expert in her field. The project was evaluated quantitatively by the number of and type of programs and services delivered to schools, number of children served, number of teachers trained in arts integration techniques, number of schools hosting pilot programs, and the number of hours of programs and services. A random sampling of teachers and students participating in the program was used to ascertain positive changes in school attendance and test scores, as well as decreased numbers of disciplinary actions and referrals. Qualitative evaluation involved responses to age- and language-appropriate questionnaires for students; teacher, school administrator, and parent surveys; and observations of program activities by key project personnel.

"I cannot say enough about the generosity and vision of the Robert and Janice McNair Foundation and its Executive Director Joanie Haley," said Mr. Wiley. "Over the years, many well-meaning education initiatives have failed because they were abandoned after a few years for a variety of reasons, lack of sustaining funding being chief among them. The McNair Foundation, Houston ISD's Northwest District administration, and our arts partners know that one must stay the course in order to see measurable results. This is especially true in the arts. Exposure to the arts affects people in evolutionary stages, something that cannot easily be measured as yearly progress on a standardized test. The indirect effect is there. You just have to know how to look for it."

AEM is a success story about building partnerships, bringing key stakeholders together, and facilitating discussions to build consensus over time—all with keeping the needs of inner-city children in mind. The power of AEM is in the belief that the arts are *essential* to the quality of life, both in and out of school, not a "frill" or an "extra." "At the end of the day," stated Mr. Wiley, "we (AEM) must be the advocates for our children and their families for arts education. If we don't speak out for them, who will?"

About the Author

Johanna M. Lockhart has extensive experience in marketing and public relations in the private sector. For more than ten years, she used that experience in her position as manager of the Department of Marketing and Business Development at the Houston Independent School District. Ms. Lockhart has created and presented marketing workshops to hundreds of school and district administrators and has made presentations at state and national conferences.

In 2014, Ms. Lockhart retired from the school district and is now launching a new endeavor. Her website, marketyourschool.net, is a result of feedback from readers of the first edition of the book. The goal is to provide marketing assistance, through consulting and workshops, to public, private, charter, or parochial schools anywhere in the country or abroad.

Ms. Lockhart holds a bachelor of arts, magna cum laude, in languages and has studied in England, Germany, Spain, and Mexico. She also holds a master of arts in communication/public relations.

Ms. Lockhart now resides in Austin, Texas. She may be reached through her website, marketyourschool.net.

Printed in Great Britain
by Amazon